nos Amis

Test Booklet

french 1

FOR CURRICULUM DEVELOPMENT

 HBJ Harcourt Brace Jovanovich, Publishers

Orlando   New York   Chicago   San Diego   Atlanta   Dallas

Requests for permission to make copies of any part of the work should be mailed to:
Permissions
Harcourt Brace Jovanovich, Publishers
Orlando, Florida 32887

PICTURE CREDITS: Positions are shown left to right and top to bottom in ascending numerical order.

TEXT PHOTOS: All photos by Pierre Capretz except page 4 bottom right, HBJ Photo; 51: HBJ Photo; 53: #1 HBJ Photo; 59: P. Courtault; 70: all photos except #17, #19 Patrick Courtault; 84: P. Courtault; 90: P. Courtault; 94: all photos except Le Louvre: Mark Antman, Le Louvre: Stephen Colwell; 105: P. Courtault; 114: #15 P. Courtault; 116: all photos except top left: P. Courtault; 132: #11 P. Courtault, #12 K. D. Franke/Peter Arnold, #13 W. Hamilton/Shostal, #14 H. Lanks/Monkmeyer, #15 G. Torton/Photos Researchers; 133: P. Courtault; 134: Courtault; 137: S. Colwell; 146: P. Courtault.

ART CREDITS: All art by Manny Haller/Zoran Orlic except page 2, HBJ; 8: HBJ; 32: Don Crews; 62: HBJ; 66: Ex. #14 Mike Vivo; 68: HBJ; 87: HBJ; 89: HBJ; 110: top: Mike Vivo; bottom: Don Crews; 112: HBJ; 120: HBJ.

Printed in the United States of America

ISBN 0-15-381844-1

® Registered Trademark, Harcourt Brace Jovanovich, Inc.

Contents

PART 1

Listening Comprehension Tests

3. You will hear five statements. Each statement is about one of the cities listed below. Listen carefully, look at the map, and write the number of each statement next to the name of the city it describes.
5 points

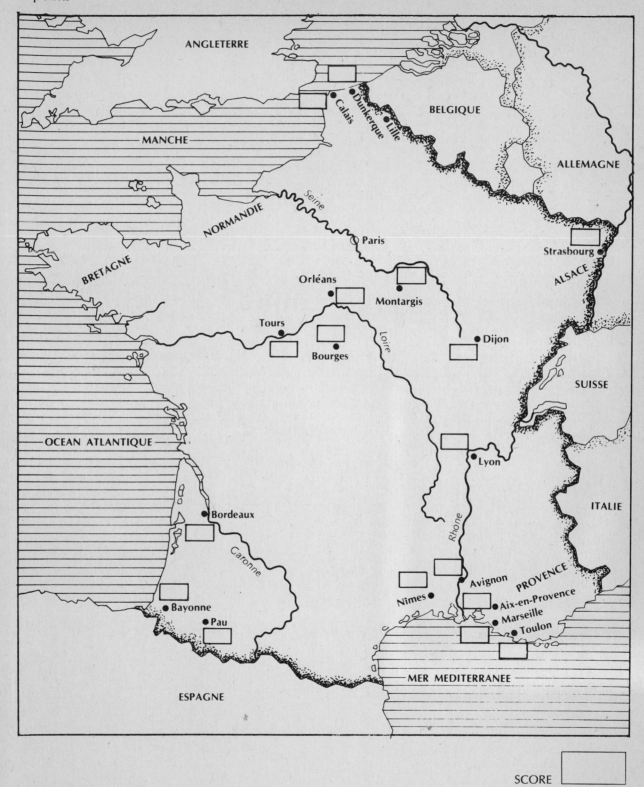

SCORE

Listening Test after Unit 1

1. Let's see how good you are at identifying boys' and girls' names and ages. You will hear eight statements. Each one contains the name and age of either a girl or a boy whom you do not know. Listen carefully. Then, for each sentence you hear, write the age in the appropriate row. For example, you hear: **Elle s'appelle Caroline; elle a sept ans.** So you write the number seven in the row labeled **"Filles."**
16 points

	Ex.	1	2	3	4	5	6	7	8
Filles	7								
Garçons									

SCORE [   ]

2. Listen carefully and write the necessary words to complete the following sentences.
4 points

1. _____ s'appelle Jean.

2. Comment s'appelle-t-_____?

3. Quel âge a-t-_____?

4. _____ habite à Paris.

SCORE [   ]

Listening Test after Unit 2

1. You will hear ten statements. Each one will be about a girl, Sylvie, or about a boy, Arnaud, or about two girls, Caroline and Christine, or about a girl and a boy, Doris and Danou. For each statement you hear, place a check mark in the appropriate row. For example, you hear: **Il a 13 ans.** You place your check mark in the row showing Arnaud because that statement is about a boy.
10 points

	Ex.	1	2	3	4	5	6	7	8	9	10
	✔										

SCORE ⬚

2. In front of you are six photographs relating to six different sports. You will hear ten statements. Write the number of each statement under the picture that suggests the sport most likely referred to.

10 points

_____ _____   _____ _____   _____ _____

_____ _____   _____ _____   _____ _____

SCORE ☐

Listening Test after Unit 3

1. You will hear three sentences. They are printed on your answer sheet, but some of the words and endings are missing. After you hear each sentence, complete the written sentence. You will have to provide the "noun marker" like **ce, ces,** or **cette,** and will have to fill in the "s" at the end of a plural noun.
6 points

1. J'aime beaucoup _____ fille _____.

2. Elle aime beaucoup _____ revue.

3. J'aime _____ livre.

SCORE [   ]

2. Here again you will hear sentences that are partially reproduced on your answer sheet. After you hear each sentence, fill in the missing parts. Here you will have to pay special attention to the verb endings and the marks of the plural.
8 points

1. J'aime tricoter. Toi aussi, tu _____?

2. Tu _____ _____ _____?

3. J'_____ _____ _____

_____.

SCORE [   ]

3. Sylvie, Philippe, Catherine, and Arnaud have been playing three rounds of a game of cards. We will give you their scores for each round. Write them on the tally sheet.
12 points

	Sylvie	Philippe	Catherine	Arnaud
First round				
Second round				
Third round				

SCORE [   ]

4. In front of you are six pictures. You will hear four sentences. Indicate to which picture each sentence refers by writing the number of the sentence under the proper picture.
4 points

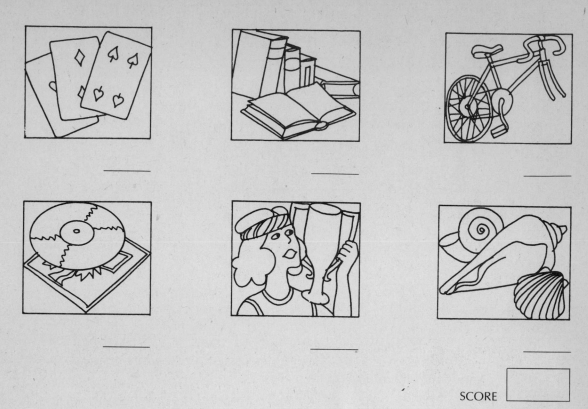

SCORE

Listening Test after Unit 4

1. You have in front of you eight pictures of clocks, each one showing a different time. You will hear eight statements, identified by the letters A through H. Each statement indicates the time shown by one of the clocks. Write the letter of each statement under the proper clock.
4 points

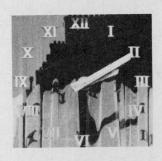

_____ _____ _____ _____

_____ _____ _____ _____

SCORE ☐

2. In front of you is a schedule blank for a French school. Imagine you are a student in this French school. You will be given a schedule for your English and French classes. Write it down in the schedule blank. For each period, you will have to write the subject matter (either **anglais** or **français**), the time, and the room number. Your Monday schedule, including your first French class, has been partially filled out to serve as a model. Here we go!
12 points

EMPLOI DU TEMPS DU 2ᵉ TRIMESTRE

HORAIRE	LUNDI	HORAIRE	MARDI	HORAIRE	MERCREDI
8 à 9	français SALLE: 25		SALLE:		SALLE:
9 à 10	maths SALLE: 9		SALLE:		SALLE:
10 à 11	histoire SALLE:		SALLE:		SALLE:
11 à 12	latin SALLE:		SALLE:		SALLE:
	SALLE:		SALLE:		SALLE:
2 à 3	dessin SALLE:		SALLE:		SALLE:
	SALLE:		SALLE:		SALLE:
4 à 5	musique SALLE:		SALLE:		SALLE:
	SALLE:		SALLE:		SALLE:

HORAIRE	JEUDI	HORAIRE	VENDREDI	HORAIRE	SAMEDI
	SALLE:		SALLE:		SALLE:
	SALLE:		SALLE:		SALLE:
	SALLE:		SALLE:		SALLE:
	SALLE:		SALLE:		SALLE:
	SALLE:		SALLE:		SALLE:
	SALLE:		SALLE:		SALLE:
	SALLE:		SALLE:		SALLE:
	SALLE:		SALLE:		SALLE:
	SALLE:		SALLE:		SALLE:

SCORE

Listening Test after Unit 4 (continued)

3. You will hear four sentences that have something to do with school. On your answer sheet are five sentences. For each sentence you hear, pick the written sentence that would follow most logically. Indicate your choice by writing the number of the spoken sentence next to the proper written sentence.
4 points

_____ Allons au réfectoire!

_____ C'est mercredi.

_____ Regardez la photo à la page 16.

_____ Levez la main.

_____ Corrigez les fautes d'orthographe.

SCORE [   ]

4. You will hear a French student who at times is talking to Mlle Dubois, a teacher, and at other times to Françoise, a classmate and friend. For each sentence you hear, decide whether the student is talking to Mlle Dubois or to Françoise and check the proper box.
3 points

Florence parle à	1	2	3	4	5	6
Mlle Dubois (le professeur d'anglais)						
Françoise (une amie de son âge)						

SCORE [   ]

5. You will hear six sentences about various boys and girls. Indicate whether each sentence you hear is about a boy or a girl by checking the proper box in the grid.
3 points

	1	2	3	4	5	6
une fille						
un garçon						

SCORE

6. You have in front of you eight pictures of school objects. You will hear eight statements about school objects. Write the number of each statement you hear next to the picture to which it refers.
4 points

SCORE

Listening Test after Unit 5

1. You will hear seven questions. On your answer sheet are seven answers. For each question you hear, select the answer that seems most appropriate. Indicate your choice by writing the number of the question next to the answer you have selected.
7 points

_____ Oui.

_____ Un film policier.

_____ Au cinéma, à Dieppe.

_____ Dans vingt minutes.

_____ En voiture.

_____ Avec des amis.

_____ Parce que nous n'avons pas classe.

SCORE [   ]

2. This is a dictation exercise. You will hear a little dialog that is printed, with words missing, on your answer sheet. Complete the text of the dialog as you hear it. First listen to the whole dialog.
6 points

—Alors, on _____?

—Oui... Tu as de l'_____? Combien est-ce que tu as?

—J'ai _____ _____. Qu'est-ce qu'on

_____?

—Eh bien, pour moi, un sandwich au _____.

SCORE [   ]

3. You will hear someone offering you various kinds of things to eat or drink. You must refuse everything, but each time you must answer by giving an appropriate reason. The grid in front of you has two possible answers: **Non merci, je n'ai pas soif,** and **Non merci, je n'ai pas faim.** For each question you hear, select the correct answer and place a check mark in the appropriate box.
6 points

	1	2	3	4	5	6
Non merci, je n'ai pas soif.						
Non merci, je n'ai pas faim.						

SCORE ☐

4. You will hear six very short exchanges. In each, someone will be offered something, and will then select something to eat or drink. In front of you are eight pictures that include the six items selected. For each exchange you hear, indicate the item by writing its number next to the appropriate picture.
6 points

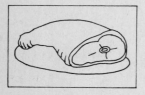

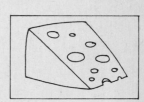

_____   _____   _____   _____

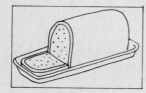

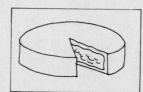

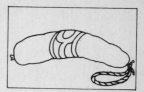

_____   _____   _____   _____

SCORE ☐

Listening Test after Unit 6

1. You will hear a short exchange twice. Just listen the first time to get an idea of what is said. The second time around, write down what you hear. (You have part of the text in front of you; just fill in what's missing.)
15 points

—_____ _____, _____ _____ _____, moi, _____!

—Ça _____ _____, moi _____!

—_____ _____ _____ _____ sandwiches!

—Oui. Un sandwich au _____ pour moi! Et toi?

—Et pour moi, deux sandwiches au _____!

SCORE [   ]

2. You will hear a conversation between two boys, Arnaud and Eric, who are trying to make a telephone call. You will be asked to answer ten easy questions on what you hear. You have the ten answers in front of you. Select the most appropriate answer for each question you hear, and write the number of the question next to the selected answer.
10 points

_____ 252-35-60   _____ C'est occupé.

_____ Dans l'appareil   _____ Elle est sortie.

_____ Dans l'annuaire   _____ Il décroche.

_____ Au fond de la salle   _____ Il fait le numéro.

_____ Les pièces   _____ Il raccroche.

SCORE [   ]

Listening Test after Unit 7

1. You will hear a short exchange twice. The first time, just listen. The second time around, write down what you hear. (You have part of the text in front of you; just fill in what's missing.)
5 points

—Qui c'est, ça, sur la photo?

—C'est un de _____ _____. Il habite aux _____.

—Ce n'est pas _____!

—_____ _____!

—Il _____ à ta sœur.

—Oui, mais lui, il a _____ _____ _____.

SCORE [   ]

2. You will hear eight statements, some about a girl, others about a boy. For each statement you hear, indicate whether it is about a girl or a boy by placing a check mark in the row labeled **"fille"** or in the row labeled **"garçon."**
8 points

	1	2	3	4	5	6	7	8
fille								
garçon								

SCORE [   ]

3. You will hear four short passages. Each refers to one member or another of the Lardan family. For each passage you hear, indicate to whom it most likely refers by placing a check mark in the proper box. You will have to select from among the father, Monsieur Lardan; the mother, Madame Lardan; Catherine; Catherine's grandmother; and the dog, Toupie.
4 points

	1	2	3	4
Monsieur Lardan				
Madame Lardan				
Catherine				
La grand-mère de Catherine				
Toupie, le chien				

SCORE [ ]

4. You will hear a conversation between Claire Poirier and her friend Arnaud. They are at Claire's house, and Arnaud has just noticed a photograph on the piano. Claire and Arnaud then talk about different members of Claire's family. Listen carefully and try to figure out who's who so that you can answer the questions in front of you by placing a check mark in the proper column. Let's read the questions together so that you will know what to look for.
8 points

	Denise	Tante Henriette	Tante Jacqueline
1. Comment s'appelle la sœur de Claire?			
2. Qui est-ce qui ressemble à Denise?			
3. Qui est-ce qui est rousse?			
4. Qui est-ce qui est la plus grande, Denise ou Tante Henriette?			
5. Qui est-ce qui est la plus jeune, Tante Henriette ou la mère de Claire?			
6. Qui est-ce qui habite à Paris?			
7. Qui est-ce qui est médecin?			
8. Qui est-ce qui est dentiste?			

SCORE [ ]

Listening Test after Unit 8

1. You will hear three merchants talking about the price of what they sell. (Pictures of these items are on your answer sheet.) Indicate the price of each item on its corresponding price tag. Note that the price is already indicated for the items shown in the examples. You have 12 price tags to fill in. 12 points

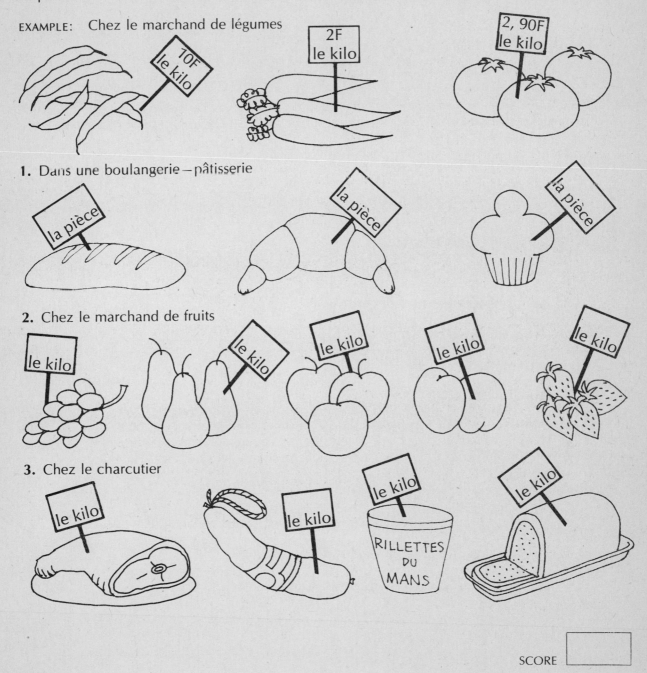

EXAMPLE: Chez le marchand de légumes

10F le kilo   2F le kilo   2, 90F le kilo

1. Dans une boulangerie—pâtisserie

la pièce   la pièce   la pièce

2. Chez le marchand de fruits

le kilo   le kilo   le kilo   le kilo   le kilo

3. Chez le charcutier

le kilo   le kilo   le kilo   le kilo

RILLETTES DU MANS

SCORE _____

2. You will hear four sentences that were said during a meal. You see in front of you five suggested rejoinders. For each sentence you hear, indicate the best rejoinder by placing a check mark in the proper box.
4 points

	1	2	3	4
—Non, de l'eau minérale.				
—Non, je préfère le gruyère.				
—Si, mais il y a trop de vinaigre!				
—Oui, donne-moi un peu d'eau.				
—Mais on n'a pas encore mangé le dessert!				

SCORE [ ]

3. You will now hear four sentences about shopping. In front of you are five suggested rejoinders. For each sentence you hear, indicate the best rejoinder by placing a check mark in the proper box.
4 points

	1	2	3	4
—Non, je n'aime pas l'agneau!				
—Non, elles sont trop chères. Prends des pommes.				
—Oui, prends une baguette et des croissants.				
—Oui, on va faire une omelette.				
—Bon, alors, achète un bifteck.				

SCORE [ ]

4. You will hear the names of 15 different foods or drinks. These names will be said rather quickly. In front of you, five categories are listed: **hors-d'œuvre, plat de viande, plat de légumes, dessert, boisson.** Indicate in which category each spoken item belongs. Place a check mark in the proper box.
15 points

	1	2	3	4	5	6	7	8	9	10	11	12	13	14	15
hors-d'œuvre															
plat de viande															
plat de légumes															
dessert															
boisson															

SCORE [ ]

Listening Test after Unit 9

1. You will hear 16 sentences. Some refer to the past, some to the present, others to the future. Listen carefully to each sentence and indicate whether it refers to the past, the present, or the future by placing a check mark in the appropriate row.
16 points

	1	2	3	4	5	6	7	8	9	10	11	12	13	14	15	16
present																
past																
future																

SCORE

2. You will hear nine statements. For each statement you hear, decide what or whom it is about. Indicate your choice by placing a check mark in the appropriate row.
9 points

	1	2	3	4	5	6	7	8	9
le sous-sol									
un pantalon									
un disque									
un électrophone									
des sandwiches									
de la limonade									
Philippe									

SCORE

Listening Test after Unit 10

1. You will hear 15 sentences. Some refer to a girl, Marie-Paule. Some refer to a boy, Jérôme. Others refer to a girl and a boy, Christine and Denis. For each sentence you hear, indicate to whom it refers by placing a check mark in the appropriate column.
15 points

	1	2	3	4	5	6	7	8	9	10	11	12	13	14	15
Marie-Paule															
Jérôme															
Christine et Denis															

SCORE

2. You will hear ten fragments of conversation. Indicate what they most probably refer to by placing a check mark in the appropriate box.
10 points

	1	2	3	4	5	6	7	8	9	10
un guide										
une rue										
une piscine										
un immeuble										
un appartement										
un ascenseur										
une chambre										

SCORE ☐

3. You will hear five questions and answers about one or several boys and girls. On your answer sheet are the incomplete answers. Write in the missing word for each. Pay special attention to the ending, which may change to show whether one girl, one boy, or several girls and boys are involved.
5 points

1. —Oui, je les ai _____ très sympathiques.

2. —Non, nous ne les avons pas _____.

3. —Non, je l'ai _____ à la piscine, tout à l'heure.

4. —Non, son père l'a _____ à Paris.

5. —Oui, je les ai _____ à la Maison des Jeunes.

SCORE ☐

Listening Test after Unit 11

1. You will hear two people talking about places where they went in Paris. The places are shown in the photographs in front of you. For each fragment of the conversation you hear, indicate which place it most probably refers to by writing its number under the appropriate photograph.
8 points

_____   _____   _____   _____

_____   _____   _____   _____

SCORE [   ]

2. You will hear eight sentences. Indicate the verb used in each spoken sentence by placing a check mark in the appropriate box.
8 points

	1	2	3	4	5	6	7	8
voir								
avoir								
aller								
faire								
être								

SCORE [   ]

3. You will hear 14 sentences. For each sentence you hear, indicate whether the verb is in the present or in the past by placing a check mark in the appropriate box.
14 points

	1	2	3	4	5	6	7	8	9	10	11	12	13	14
present														
past														

SCORE

Listening Test after Unit 12

1. You will be given the date of birth of five boys and girls whose names you see in front of you. Write down the date of birth of each boy and girl. Use figures for the day and year, but spell out the name of the month.
15 points

1. Monique: _____ _____ _____ _____

2. Jean-Luc: _____ _____ _____

3. Anne-Marie: _____ _____ _____

4. Marie-Odile: _____ _____ _____

5. Patrick: _____ _____ _____

SCORE ☐

2. You will hear 15 sentences. Indicate whether each sentence you hear refers to the past, the present, or the future by placing a check mark in the appropriate box.
15 points

	1	2	3	4	5	6	7	8	9	10	11	12	13	14	15
past															
present															
future															

SCORE ☐

Listening Test after Unit 13

1. You will hear 15 utterances. Identify each utterance you hear with one of the ten that you have printed in front of you. Indicate your choice by placing a check mark in the appropriate box. 15 points

	1	2	3	4	5	6	7	8	9	10	11	12	13	14	15
Ils sont seize à table!															
Ils sont six à table!															
Elle a beaucoup de pain.															
Elle a beaucoup de peine.															
C'est dans le Maine.															
C'est dans la main.															
Vous connaissez l'île de Sein?															
Vous connaissez l'île de la Seine?															
Toujours plein!															
Toujours pleine!															

SCORE

2. You will hear ten fragments of conversation. In front of you are ten photographs. Write the number of each fragment below the photograph that corresponds to it best.
10 points

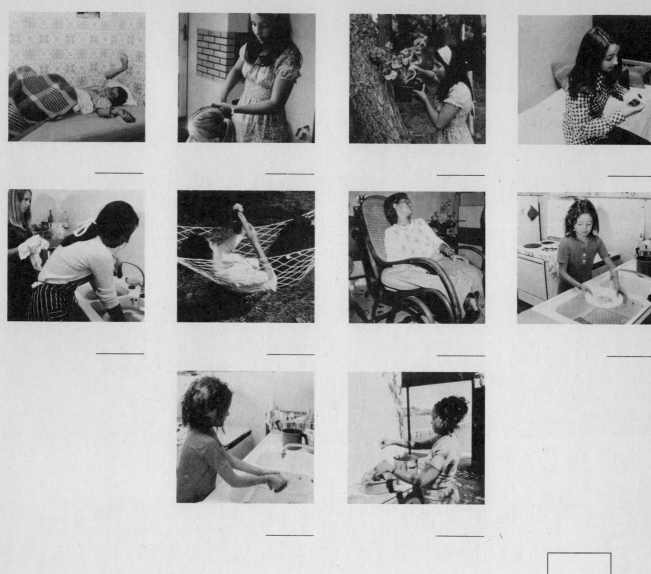

Listening Test after Unit 14

1. You will be told what instrument each of six boys and girls is playing. In front of you are the names of the boys and girls and the pictures of the instruments. Write the name of each boy or girl next to the instrument he or she plays.
6 points

Patrick, Viviane, Corinne, Marc, Isabelle, Jean-Luc

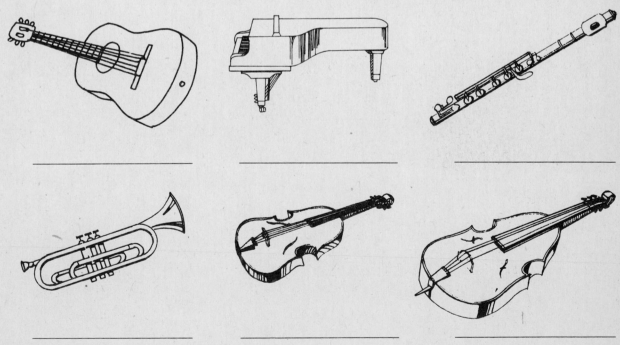

SCORE

2. You will hear fragments of conversation in groups of three. Each fragment is the first part of an exchange between two people. The second part, the rejoinder, is written on your answer sheet. For each fragment you hear, select the most likely rejoinder, and write the number of the fragment next to the appropriate rejoinder.
9 points

Group 1

_____ Tu as oublié d'appuyer sur le bouton d'enregistrement!

_____ Bien sûr le haut parleur n'est pas branché!

_____ Oui, baisse en peu!

Group 2

_____ Non, c'est celle de Jacques.

_____ Non, de la clarinette.

_____ Non, c'est un chanteur.

Group 3

_____ Eh bien, il faut le réparer!

_____ On va voir. On va faire un essai.

_____ Lequel?

SCORE [   ]

Listening Test after Unit 15

1. You will hear eight spoken items. On your answer sheet are eight printed rejoinders. For each item you hear, select the most likely rejoinder. Indicate your choice by placing a check mark in the appropriate box.
8 points

	1	2	3	4	5	6	7	8
A Oui, je suis tombée!								
B Oui, elle a cassé ses skis.								
C Non, il s'est cassé la jambe.								
D Elle s'est cassé le bras en faisant du ski.								
E Oui, le télésiège ne marche pas.								
F Non, il faut faire la queue au moins une heure!								
G Viens te réchauffer près du feu!								
H Non, il n'y a pas de neige.								

SCORE

2. You will hear someone who wants to take up skiing and who is trying to figure out how much the equipment will cost. Listen for the name of each item that will be bought. Look up its price on the page of the catalog reproduced on your sheet. Then put the price in the proper space under the heading "Budget."
6 points

80 F

Budget

1 _____

2 _____

3 _____

4 _____

5 _____

6 _____

total: 875 F

300 F

475 F

30 F

200 F

40 F

50 F

225 F

45 F

35 F

250 F

3. You will hear a conversation between Alain and Patrick. You will then hear six questions. For each, you will select an answer from among those you see printed on your sheet.
6 points

	1	2	3	4	5	6
Il a encore mal à la jambe.						
Il est tombé.						
Il a travaillé.						
Il a fait du ski.						
Il a loué des skis.						
Il a pris le bus.						

Listening Test after Unit 16

1. You will hear a conversation between a visitor and old grandfather Bouvier. The conversation will be interrupted from time to time by questions. Select the most likely answers among those which you see printed in front of you. Indicate your choice by writing the number of the question next to the most likely answer.
18 points

_____ _____ _____ au pré   _____ _____ _____ la maison

_____ _____ _____ au champ   _____ _____ _____ la cuisine

_____ _____ _____ au jardin   _____ _____ _____ de la paille

_____ _____ _____ à l'étable   _____ _____ _____ le voisin

_____ _____ _____ à la grange   _____ _____ _____ le blé

_____ _____ _____ sous le hangar   _____ _____ _____ le tracteur

DISCARD

_____ _____ _____ les foins

_____ _____ _____ les moutons

_____ _____ _____ les vaches

_____ _____ _____ des tomates

SCORE [   ]

2. You will hear someone talking about what Petit Louis has been doing this morning. You have in front of you a drawing representing Petit Louis and the animals he has been feeding. As you listen, trace a line showing where Petit Louis went and in which order. You may use numbers (1, 2, 3, 4) to indicate the sequence clearly.
4 points

SCORE ____

3. You will hear six sentences. Indicate whether they refer to the present or the past by placing a check mark in the appropriate box.
3 points

	1	2	3	4	5	6
present						
past						

SCORE ____

Listening Test after Unit 17

1. You will hear Doris and Claude talking about the pictures which you see reproduced in front of you. Write the number of each fragment of conversation you hear under the picture it refers to. 8 points

SCORE

2. You will hear seventeen sentences, some of which refer to the present, others to the past. Indicate whether each sentence you hear is in the present or in the past by placing a check mark in the appropriate box.

17 points

	1	2	3	4	5	6	7	8	9	10	11	12	13	14	15	16	17
present																	
past																	

SCORE _____

Listening Test after Unit 18

1. You will hear fourteen incomplete fragments of conversation. The last part of each fragment is printed on your test sheet, but there is one word missing. You will have to write this word in, choosing from the list you have in front of you. (You may use a word more than once.)
14 points

bête — bêtes — fête — fêter — hâte — hôtes — mâts — pâte — pâté — pâtes — râpé

1. Il faut s'occuper des _____ tous les jours!

2. Nos _____ nous ont très bien reçus.

3. ... pour _____ son anniversaire.

4. On va y mettre du fromage _____.

5. C'est la _____ des mères, aujourd'hui.

6. Elle n'est pas _____ du tout.

7. Nous étions à la _____ du village.

8. Mais ce que je n'aime pas ce sont les petites _____ qui rentrent dans la tente et qui courent partout.

9. C'est la _____ nationale!

10. Voilà du _____.

11. Il avait trois _____, un grand et deux plus petits.

12. Je n'ai pas de _____ dentifrice!

13. Je n'aime pas les _____.

14. Il est parti en _____.

SCORE [　　]

2. You will hear François talking about what he did at camp. You see six pictures which refer to what François is talking about. Write the number of each passage you hear under the picture which it refers to.
6 points

_____   _____   _____

_____   _____   _____

SCORE [   ]

Listening Test after Unit 19

1. You will hear eleven statements. Decide whether each one refers to a friend, a boat, or a plane. Place your check mark in the appropriate box.
11 points

	1	2	3	4	5	6	7	8	9	10	11
notre ami											
notre bateau											
l'avion d'Air France											

SCORE ☐

2. You will hear nine statements about nine different people. Try to decide what the nationality of each person most likely is. Write a simple answer like: **Elle est française,** or **Il est tunisien.**
9 points

1. _____

2. _____

3. _____

4. _____

5. _____

6. _____

7. _____

8. _____

9. _____

SCORE ☐

Listening Test after Unit 20

1. You will hear eight questions. You see on your test sheet four possible answers — A, B, C, D. For each question you hear, select the most likely answer and place a check mark in the appropriate box.
8 points

	1	2	3	4	5	6	7	8
A Mme Slim								
B le mouton								
C midi								
D le commerce								

SCORE [   ]

2. You will hear twelve sentences. You see on your test sheet six printed sentences. For each sentence you hear, select the printed sentence which would most likely follow it. Place a check mark in the appropriate box.
12 points

	1	2	3	4	5	6	7	8	9	10	11	12
A Il n'y a rien à manger dans la maison!												
B Il n'y a rien pour éplucher les légumes!												
C Il n'y a rien pour faire cuire les légumes!												
D Je n'ai rien à mettre pour sortir!												
E Je n'ai rien pour mettre mon argent!												
F Il faut faire réparer tes chaussures!												

SCORE [   ]

Listening Test after Unit 21

1. You will hear six short sentences. You see in front of you six pictures. Write the number of each sentence you hear under the picture it most likely refers to.
6 points

SCORE

2. You will hear eight incomplete sentences by people talking about a traveling fair. Complete each. You see in front of you eight words. Write the number of each incomplete sentence you hear next to the word which would best complete it.
8 points

_____ chance

_____ plaire

_____ bleus

_____ vertige

_____ carton

_____ tamponneuses

_____ cache

_____ froussard

SCORE

3. You will hear six fragments of conversation about a traveling fair. For each fragment you hear, indicate what it most likely refers to by placing a check mark in the appropriate box.
6 points

	1	2	3	4	5	6
la grande roue						
les autos tamponneuses						
le tir						
le fakir						
la loterie						

SCORE ☐

Listening Test after Unit 22

1. You will hear directions to perform eight gymnastic exercises. You have in front of you eight drawings identified by the letters A through H. For each set of directions you hear, find the corresponding drawing. Indicate your choice by writing the number of the set of directions under the corresponding drawing.
8 points

A _____   B _____   C _____   D _____

E _____   F _____   G _____   H _____

SCORE [   ]

2. You will be asked to look again at the eight drawings you have just been using, and to answer questions about the different gymnastic exercises they show. The questions will bear on different parts of the body that are listed in the grid. Select those which answer each question, and indicate your choice by placing check marks in the appropriate boxes. Note that the answer to a given question may involve several parts of the body. Whenever this is the case, check as many boxes as necessary.

12 points

	1	2	3	4	5	6	7	8	9	10	11	12	13	14
la tête														
une épaule														
les épaules														
le dos														
la poitrine														
le ventre														
un bras														
les bras														
les coudes														
une main														
les mains														
une jambe														
les jambes														
les genoux														
un pied														
les pieds														

SCORE [ ]

Listening Test after Unit 23

1. You will hear fragments of conversation about choosing gifts for nine boys and girls. You see in front of you the names of the nine boys and girls and a list of the gifts considered. As you listen, indicate who is supposed to get what by tracing a line between the name of the gift and the name of the boy or girl for whom it is intended.
9 points

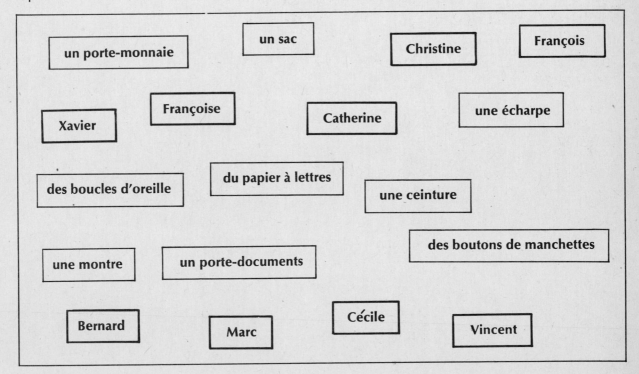

un porte-monnaie	un sac	Christine	François
Xavier	Françoise	Catherine	une écharpe
des boucles d'oreille	du papier à lettres	une ceinture	
		des boutons de manchettes	
une montre	un porte-documents		
Bernard	Marc	Cécile	Vincent

SCORE

2. You will hear a not very serious conversation between two young children. The conversation will be interrupted by eleven questions about what the children are saying. For each question you hear, choose the best answer among those which you have in front of you. Indicate your choice by placing a check mark in the appropriate box.
11 points

	1	2	3	4	5	6	7	8	9	10	11
un autre gâteau											
un bateau à voiles											
des bougies											
une bijouterie											
des cartes postales											
un rasoir électrique											
un sac à main											
dans les magasins											
dans un port											
Elle aime les fleurs.											
Il soufflerait très fort.											

SCORE ☐

Listening Test after Unit 24

1. You will hear five nouns with an article. You see those five nouns printed in front of you, but a blank space has been left at the beginning of each noun. As you hear each noun, decide whether it is spelled with an "h" at the beginning or not. Fill in the blank space with an "h" whenever necessary.
5 points

1. un _____aut-parleur

2. un _____ors-d'œuvre

3. un _____ami

4. un _____aricot

5. un _____angar

SCORE [   ]

2. You will hear ten sentences that are either in the future or in the conditional. Indicate which by placing a check mark in the appropriate box.
10 points

	1	2	3	4	5	6	7	8	9	10
Futur ... si c'est possible										
Conditionnel ... si c'était possible										

SCORE [   ]

3. You will hear five short fragments of conversation that relate to the pictures you see in front of you. For each fragment you hear, indicate to which picture it most probably relates by writing its number under the picture.
5 points

SCORE

PART 2

Reading / Writing Tests

Test after Unit 1

1. Write three sentences in French about Denise Goulet, telling her name, her age, and where she lives.
6 points

1. _____

2. _____

3. _____

SCORE ☐

2. Write three questions in French, asking a classmate his or her name, his or her age, and where he or she lives.
9 points

4. _____

5. _____

6. _____

SCORE ☐

3. Rewrite the sentences, substituting the noun in parentheses for the underlined noun. Make any necessary changes in the gender markers.
10 points
EXAMPLE: C'est un grand <u>port</u>.   (île)

_____

7. Il habite dans une <u>ville</u>.   (village)

_____

8. Qui est la <u>fille</u>?   (garçon)

_____

9. C'est un petit <u>appartement</u>.   (maison)

_____

10. C'est une <u>ville</u>.   (port)

_____

11. Elle habite dans ce grand <u>appartement</u>.   (maison)

_____

SCORE [   ]

4. Complete the following list of numbers from one to twenty.
10 points

12. _____, deux, _____, quatre, _____,

_____, sept, huit, _____, dix, _____, douze,

treize, _____, quinze, _____, dix-sept, _____,

dix-neuf, _____.

SCORE [   ]

5. Write five sentences in French about yourself. Tell your name, your age, which town or city you live in, whether it is big or small, and whether you live in an apartment or a house.
15 points

13. _____

14. _____

15. _____

16. _____

17. _____

SCORE [   ]

Test after Unit 2

1. Write sentences, telling what the people in the pictures are doing. Use a form of the verb **faire** and the correct subject pronoun, **il, ils, elle** or **elles.**
12 points

1. _____

2. _____

3. _____

4. _____

SCORE ☐

2. Identify the following sports equipment. Use the correct gender marker, **un** or **une**, with each noun. Then, write a sentence telling that the person indicated is playing the associated sport. 18 points

EXAMPLE:

un ballon (ovale)

François _joue au rugby._

5. _____

Sabine _____

6. _____

Patrick et Didier _____

7. _____

Nous _____

8. _____

Tu _____

9. _____

Vous _____

10. _____

Je _____

SCORE [   ]

Test after Unit 2 (continued)

3. Pretend that you are going to paint this picture by number. Write the colors in French. Do not use the article.
2 points

11. _____

12. _____

13. _____

14. _____

SCORE [   ]

4. Fill in the correct form of the verb in parentheses.
10 points

EXAMPLE: (aimer) Il _____*aime*_____ le football.

15. (rentrer) Nous _____ avec Claire.

16. (regarder) Qu'est-ce que vous _____?

17. (regarder) Je _____ la télé.

18. (habiter) Est-ce que tu _____ à Paris?

19. (trouver) Louise _____ le ski trop dangereux.

20. (parler) Richard et Arnaud _____.

21. (aimer) Tu _____ mieux le ski ou le cheval?

22. (rentrer) Vous _____? Pourquoi?

23. (habiter) Elles _____ aux Etats-Unis.

24. (trouver) Nous _____ ça amusant.

SCORE [   ]

5. Write sentences, answering the following questions about yourself.
8 points

25. Qu'est-ce que tu fais comme sports?

_____

26. Qu'est-ce que tu regardes comme sports à la télé?

_____

27. Qu'est-ce que tu aimes comme sports?

_____

28. Tu trouves ça amusant, le ski?

_____

SCORE [   ]

Test after Unit 3

1. Write sentences, using the correct form of the verb **avoir** and the pictured noun. (Use the gender marker **un** or **une** before each noun.)
12 points

1. Pierre / avoir

_____

2. tu / avoir /

_____

3. nous / avoir /

_____

4. Sylvie et Philippe / avoir /

_____

5. je / avoir /

_____

6. vous / avoir /

_____

SCORE [   ]

2. Fill in the correct form of the verb **être.**
6 points

7. Nous _____ aux Etats-Unis.

8. Dieppe _____ un port.

9. Est-ce que vous _____ photographe amateur?

10. Sabine et Sylvie _____ collectionneuses.

11. Tu _____ sûre?

12. Je ne _____ pas dans cette équipe.   SCORE [   ]

3. Write the plural of the gender marker and the pictured noun.
5 points

13. le   _____

14. cette   _____

15. ce   _____

16. un   _____

17. la   _____   SCORE [   ]

4. Write out the following numbers.
4 points

18. 65 _____   22. 96 _____

19. 51 _____   23. 410 _____

20. 83 _____   24. 48 _____

21. 74 _____   25. 107 _____

SCORE [   ]

Test after Unit 3 (continued)

5. Above each picture is a question about it. Below each picture you are to: (a) write a negative answer to the question, and (b) write a sentence that tells the correct information according to the picture.
8 points

EXAMPLE: Il fait de la photo?

Non, il ne fait pas de photo.

Il lit une revue.

Elles réparent le vélo?

26. Non, _____

_____

27. _____

Il bricole?

28. Non, _____

_____

29. _____

Les filles tricotent?

30. Non, _____

_____

31. _____

Les jeunes écoutent la radio?

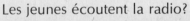
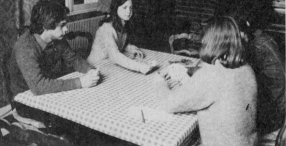

32. Non, _____

_____

33. _____

SCORE ☐

6. Complete the sentences, using words from the list below.
5 points

simple	cœurs	marque	gagner	mal
photos	jeu	lit	perdre	plage

34. Catherine _____ les points.

35. Philippe a 25 points seulement! Il est en train de _____!

36. Arnaud joue bien, mais Sylvie joue _____.

37. Sylvie a tous les cœurs; elle est en train de _____.

38. Qui a tous les _____?

39. Danou trouve les coquillages à la _____.

40. J'aime ces _____. Elles sont extraordinaires!

41. L'appareil-photo de Doris est très _____.

42. Philippe _____ des livres.

43. Je veux jouer aux échecs. Tu as un _____ d'échecs?

SCORE ☐

7. Write five sentences, telling about your leisure-time activities. For example, do you have a camera? Do you like to take pictures? Are you a collector? Of what? Do you watch TV? Do you listen to records or cassettes? Do you play games? What do you like to read?
10 points

44. _____

45. _____

46. _____

47. _____

48. _____

SCORE ☐

Test after Unit 4

1. Write sentences, using the words in the given order. Make any necessary changes in the words and add other words that are needed.
10 points

1. François / aller / gymnase

_____

2. nous / aller / bureaux

_____

3. est-ce que / tu / aller / bibliothèque?

_____

4. François et le nouveau / aller / abri pour bicyclettes

_____

5. vous / aller / réfectoire?

_____

SCORE [ ]

2. Complete the sentences, using the preposition **de** and a definite article. (Use contractions if necessary.)
4 points

6. Le gymnase est au fond _____ cour.

7. Les cuisines sont à côté _____ réfectoire.

8. Le réfectoire est près _____ abri pour bicyclettes.

9. Les bureaux sont en face _____ cuisines.

SCORE [ ]

3. Write sentences, telling what time it is.
8 points

10. _____

11. _____

12. _____

13. _____

14. _____

15. _____

16. _____

17. _____

SCORE [ ]

Test after Unit 4 (continued)

4. Write commands, telling these people *to do* what they are not doing. Pay careful attention to whom you are speaking. Be sure to add the correct form of "please" (**s'il vous plaît** or **s'il te plaît**).
3 points
EXAMPLE: Arnaud ne répare pas le vélo.

Répare le vélo, s'il te plaît.
_____

18. François et Florence ne regardent pas les dessins.

_____

19. Monsieur Pujol ne corrige pas les devoirs.

_____

20. Sylvie n'efface pas le tableau.

_____

SCORE [ ]

5. Write sentences, suggesting to your friends that you do the following activities together.
3 points

EXAMPLE: (faire du ski) _____ *Faisons du ski.* _____

21. (jouer au monopoly) _____

22. (aller à la bibliothèque) _____

23. (commencer les devoirs) _____

SCORE [ ]

6. Complete the sentences, describing François' class. Choose the appropriate adjective from the list below and write its correct form in the blank.
8 points

| amusant | bon | ennuyeux | timide |
| mauvais | distrait | paresseux | doué |

24. Florence ne fait pas attention. Elle est _____.

25. Sabine a 15 en anglais et elle n'étudie pas! Elle est _____ pour les langues.

26. Arnaud ne parle pas en classe. Il est _____.

27. Les élèves aiment le professeur de dessin. Elle est très _____.

28. Catherine est intelligente, mais elle n'étudie pas. Elle est _____.

29. Philippe est _____ en orthographe. Il fait trop de fautes.

30. Sylvie est _____ en latin.

31. François n'aime pas le professeur de maths. Il trouve M. Pujol _____.

SCORE ☐

7. Write seven sentences about your own school. You should tell which school you go to, how many subjects you study, which subject(s) you like the best, the days on which you have class, what time you begin in the morning, what time you have lunch, what time you come home in the afternoon.
14 points

32. _____

33. _____

34. _____

35. _____

36. _____

37. _____

38. _____

SCORE ☐

Test after Unit 5

1. Fill in the correct form of the verb in parentheses.
6 points

    1. (partir)   Je _____ cet après-midi.

    2. (sortir)   Sylvie _____ avec Sabine?

    3. (sortir)   Oui, elles _____ .

    4. (finir)   Vous _____ vos devoirs.

    5. (finir)   Le match _____ dans une heure.

    6. (choisir)   Nous _____ un film comique.

SCORE

2. Write appropriate questions for the following conversation.
10 points

    7. _____
       —Cet après-midi? Au cinéma.

    8. _____
       —Avec Dominique et Bernard.

    9. _____
       — « Rio Bravo ». C'est un western.

   10. _____
       —A trois heures.

   11. _____
       —Catherine? Non, elle reste à la maison.

SCORE

3. Write sentences, using the given words and the picture cues to tell what kind of film the people are choosing.
10 points

12. Dominique/choisir

_____

_____

13. nous/choisir

_____

_____

14. les enfants/choisir

_____

_____

15. je/choisir

_____

_____

16. tu/choisir

_____

_____

SCORE

Test after Unit 5 (continued)

4. The following conversations take place in a café. Fill in the blanks with an appropriate indication of quantity: in general, some, or a unit.
9 points

17. —Vous voulez _____ eau minérale?

18. —Non, merci, je n'aime pas _____ eau minérale.

19. —Donnez-moi _____ limonade, s'il vous plaît.

20. —Vous avez _____ jambon?

21. —Non, il n'y a plus _____ jambon.

22. —Alors, je vais prendre _____ saucisson.

23. —Vous avez _____ la glace?

—Oui, Mademoiselle.

24. —Alors donnez-moi _____ glace à la noisette, s'il vous plaît.

25. —Nous n'avons pas _____ glace à la noisette, Mademoiselle.

SCORE [   ]

5. Rewrite the sentences, using a form of the verb **aller** to express future time. Make other necessary changes.
5 points

EXAMPLE: Je regarde la télévision.

Je vais regarder la télévision.
_____

26. Le film finit à cinq heures.

_____

27. Nous sortons cet après-midi.

_____

28. A quelle heure est-ce que tu passes chez moi?

_____

29. Ils restent avec nous.

_____

30. Vous ne payez pas l'addition?

_____

SCORE [   ]

6. Answer the following question, identifying the picture cues.
10 points

Où est-ce qu'on va? On va...

31.   32.   33.   34.

_____   _____   _____   _____

SCORE [   ]

7. The following part is optional. You may earn an extra eight points. Choose the appropriate verb and write its correct form in the blank.

choisir	laisser	commander	manger
apporter	avoir	payer	aimer

Catherine, Dominique, Bernard et Philippe _____ faim. Ils _____

aux Ambassadeurs à Dieppe. Bernard et les filles _____ un sandwich au pâté.

Philippe n'_____ pas le pâté. Il _____ un sandwich au jambon. Le

garçon _____ les sandwiches. Une fois terminé, il faut _____

l'addition. Les amis ne _____ pas de pourboire parce que le service est compris.

SCORE [   ]

Summary Test after Unit 6

1. Fill in the correct form of the verb in parentheses.
   15 points

   1. (chercher)   Evelyne _____ le numéro de téléphone.

   2. (avoir)   Catherine _____ quinze ans.

   3. (étudier)   J'_____ les maths.

   4. (choisir)   Est-ce que tu _____ le bleu ou le jaune?

   5. (bavarder)   Les élèves _____ en classe.

   6. (faire)   Je _____ du vélo cet après-midi.

   7. (finir)   Nous _____ dans une heure.

   8. (aller)   Je _____ au bowling ce soir.

   9. (compter)   Toi, tu _____ les points.

   10. (sortir)   Avec qui est-ce qu'elle _____?

   11. (téléphoner) A qui est-ce que vous _____?

   12. (écouter)   Nous _____ des disques.

   13. (partir)   Quand est-ce que tu _____?

   14. (effacer)   _____ le tableau, s'il vous plaît.

   15. (être)   Je _____ libre ce soir.

SCORE _____

2. Look at each picture and then write a question that asks for further information about the situation shown.

12 points

EXAMPLE:

Qu'est-ce qu'il lit?

16.

17.

18.

19.

20.

21.

SCORE

Summary Test after Unit 6 (continued)

3. Rewrite the sentences, adding the correct form of the verb in parentheses. Make other necessary changes.
10 points

EXAMPLE: (aimer) Nous écoutons des disques. *Nous aimons écouter des disques.*

22. (aimer) Je fais du cheval. _____

23. (aller) Nous ne jouons pas au tennis. _____

24. (aller) Les jeunes mangent au café. _____

25. (aimer) Est-ce que tu tricotes? _____

26. (aller) Vous sortez ce soir? _____

SCORE ☐

4. Fill in the correct form of the adjective in parentheses.
10 points

27. (libre) Catherine, est-ce que tu es _____ ce soir?

28. (prêt) Nous sommes _____ à partir.

29. (occupé) La ligne est _____.

30. (distrait) Arnaud et Didier sont un peu _____.

31. (doué) L'amie de François est _____ pour les maths.

32. (grand) Ils habitent dans une _____ maison.

33. (sérieux) Sylvie et Alain sont trop _____.

34. (ennuyeux) Je trouve cette histoire _____.

35. (amusant) Le film est vraiment _____.

36. (pressé) Les garçons sont _____.

SCORE ☐

5. Rewrite the sentences, replacing the underlined word with the word in parentheses. Make other necessary changes.
13 points

37. (sont)   Ce garçon <u>est</u> dans l'équipe de Montargis.

_____

38. (parle)   Elle <u>cherche</u> le professeur.

_____

39. (regarde)   Les élèves <u>regardent</u> le dessin.

_____

40. (patinoire)   Il va au <u>café</u>.

_____

41. (photo)   Tu as des <u>photos</u>?

_____

42. (cassette)   Ecoutez ces <u>cassettes</u>.

_____

43. (couloir)   Le téléphone est au fond de la <u>cour</u>.

_____

44. (annuaires / appareil)   Il y a un <u>annuaire</u> près du <u>téléphone</u>.

_____

45. (sont)   Où <u>est</u> le journal?

_____

46. (ballon)   Quel est le prix de la <u>communication</u>?

_____

47. (filles)   Dominique téléphone à la <u>fille</u>.

_____

48. (ne fait pas)   François <u>fait</u> des erreurs.

_____

SCORE [   ]

Summary Test after Unit 6 (continued)

6. Complete the conversation below. Imagine that you are French. An American tourist approaches you on the street in Paris and asks you the following questions. You help him out.
5 points

49. —Excusez-moi, Monsieur (Mademoiselle). Où est-ce qu'on peut téléphoner, s'il vous plaît?

_____

50. —C'est combien, la communication?

_____

51. —Je n'ai pas le numéro. Qu'est-ce que je fais?

_____

52. —Et pour téléphoner? Qu'est-ce que je fais?

_____

53. — Merci, Monsieur (Mademoiselle). Au revoir.

_____

SCORE [   ]

7. Complete the answers to the following questions.
5 points

54. François Le Sève va à un CES?

Oui, _____

55. Il n'étudie pas l'anglais?

Si, _____

56. François aime le latin?

Non, _____

57. Il n'a pas classe le samedi?

Si, _____

58. Et vous, vous avez classe le samedi?

Non, _____

SCORE [   ]

8. Write a telephone conversation, using the words in parentheses. You are calling your friend, Catherine Lardan. Her mother answers the phone and then puts Catherine on. You and your friend decide what to do this afternoon.
30 points

59. VOUS   *(l'appareil)* _____

_____

60. MME LARDAN   *(quittez)* _____

_____

61. VOUS   *(occupée)* _____

62. CATHERINE   *(libre)* _____

63. VOUS   *(sortir)* _____

64. CATHERINE   *(aller)* _____

65. VOUS   *(patinoire)* _____

66. CATHERINE   *(ennuyeux)* _____

67. VOUS   *(cartes)* _____

68. CATHERINE   *(viens)* _____

_____

SCORE [   ]

Test after Unit 7

1. Below is a diagram of your imaginary family. Answer the questions in complete sentences, according to your new identity. Always identify others in relationship to yourself.
10 points

EXAMPLE: Qui est Claire Marchand?

C'est ma cousine.

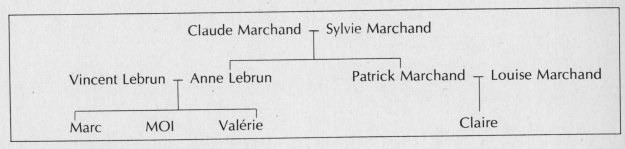

1. Qui sont Claude et Sylvie Marchand?

_____

2. Qui est Louise Marchand?

_____

3. Vous avez des frères et des sœurs? Combien?

_____

4. Qui est Patrick Marchand?

_____

5. Qui sont Anne et Vincent Lebrun?

_____

SCORE

2. Rewrite the following paragraph, making all the changes necessary so that it describes your cousin Marc.
5 points

6.   Ma cousine Valérie est grande et blonde. C'est une fille sérieuse. Elle travaille comme ouvrière dans une usine près de chez elle.

_____

_____

_____

SCORE [   ]

3. Rewrite the sentences, substituting the word in parentheses for the underlined word. Make the necessary changes in the verb and the possessive article.
10 points

7. Il attend ses amis. (ils)

_____

8. Je réponds à la lettre de ma cousine. (elle)

_____

9. Tu descends en ville avec tes camarades? (vous)

_____

10. Il perd son match de tennis. (je)

_____

11. Vous entendez votre chien? (tu)

_____

SCORE [   ]

Test after Unit 7 (continued)

4. The pictures below show occupations. Write sentences, stating each person's occupation.
5 points

12. Mlle Leclerc   13. M. Charpentier   14. M. Lebrun   15. Mme Caron   16. M. Dufour

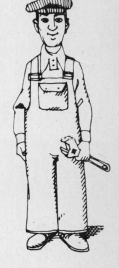

12. _____

13. _____

14. _____

15. _____

16. _____

SCORE [   ]

5. Complete the conversations, filling in the correct independent pronoun: **moi, toi, lui, elle, nous, vous, eux, elles.**
5 points

17. —Nous allons à la piscine. Et _____? —Pas _____. Je reste à la maison.

18. —Où sont Philippe et Marc? —_____? Ils sont au café.

19. —Regarde cette photo. C'est Alain? —Oui, c'est _____.

20. —Est-ce que Denise travaille? —_____? Jamais!

SCORE [   ]

6. Rewrite the sentences, putting the adjective in its correct form and place.
10 points

21. Les Lardan ont un appartement. (grand)

_____

22. Nous avons une voiture. (petit)

_____

23. Doris lit une histoire. (amusant)

_____

24. Le commerçant n'aime pas les employés. (paresseux)

_____

25. L'élève donne une réponse. (mauvais)

_____

SCORE [   ]

7. Write a negative answer to each question, using the words in parentheses.
5 points

26. Est-ce que vous entendez les oiseaux? (ne... rien)

Non, _____

27. Est-ce que le grand-père de Catherine travaille? (ne... plus)

Non, _____

28. Est-ce que les Lardan vont quelquefois à la Martinique? (ne... jamais)

Non, _____

29. Nous avons des balles et des raquettes? (ne... ni... ni)

Non, _____

30. Est-ce qu'elle a un album? (ne... pas)

Non, _____

SCORE [   ]

Test after Unit 8

1. Identify the pictures of fruit or vegetables. Then complete each sentence, using the appropriate pronoun.
5 points

EXAMPLE:

des pommes de terre
_____

Elles
_____ coûtent combien?

1.

_____

_____ sont très bonnes.

2.

_____

_____ est délicieux.

3.

_____

_____ sont trop chers.

4.

_____

_____ est bien mûre.

5.

_____

_____ coûtent 2,25 F la pièce.

SCORE [   ]

2. Write sentences, using the given words and picture cues. Use the correct verb form and the appropriate expression of quantity with the nouns shown.
15 points

4. Rewrite the sentences, using the indirect object pronoun **lui** or **leur**.
10 points

EXAMPLE: Mme Giuliani donne de l'argent à Jean-Marcel.

Mme Giuliani lui donne de l'argent.

16. M. Giuliani passe les fromages à Mme Giuliani.

_____

17. Jean-Marcel apporte le dessert à ses parents.

_____

18. Passe les hors-d'œuvre à ton grand-père!

_____

19. Donnez des frites à vos cousins!

_____

20. Est-ce que tu vas verser de l'eau à ta cousine?

_____

SCORE [   ]

5. Write five short sentences, choosing from the cues below. Your sentences should say that: you go grocery shopping—you go to the butcher and the baker—you buy meat and bread—you prepare lunch—you make steaks and French fries—your brother sets the table—you both eat lunch with your parents.
10 points

21. _____

22. _____

23. _____

24. _____

25. _____

SCORE [   ]

Test after Unit 9

1. Change the verbs in the following paragraph to the passé composé. Write the verb forms in the spaces provided below.
10 points

(C'est M. Lardan qui parle.)

Ma fille Catherine et son frère donnent[1] une surprise-partie. Ils invitent[2] une douzaine de leurs copains. Philippe range[3] la pièce et Catherine choisit[4] les disques. Mme Lardan et moi, nous aidons[5] bien sûr. Elle, elle fait[6] des sandwiches au jambon et des gâteaux. Moi, je vérifie[7] l'électrophone et, après, je descends[8] une table. La surprise-partie a[9] lieu dans le sous-sol. Voilà! Tout est[10] extraordinaire!

1. _____   5. _____   8. _____

2. _____   6. _____   9. _____

3. _____   7. _____   10. _____

4. _____

SCORE [   ]

2. Identify the pictures of jewelry or clothing. Use the indefinite article **un, une,** or **des** before each noun.
6 points

11.

12.

13.

_____   _____   _____

14.

15.

16.

_____   _____   _____

SCORE [   ]

3. Imagine that you have just returned from a party. Describe the party by writing two sentences about each picture. The verbs must be in the passé composé.
12 points

17.

_____

_____

_____

_____

18.

_____

_____

_____

_____

19.

_____

_____

_____

_____

SCORE ☐

Test after Unit 9 (continued)

4. You and your friend are discussing preparations for a party. Answer each question affirmatively, using the pronoun **en** in your response.
10 points

EXAMPLE: Pierre va apporter du pâté?

Oui, il va en apporter.

20. Tu vas acheter des chips?

_____

21. Corine va apporter du Coca-Cola?

_____

22. Brigitte a des disques?

_____

23. Ta mère a préparé des sandwiches?

_____

24. Et moi, j'apporte de la limonade?

_____

SCORE ☐

5. Write sentences in the present tense, using the given words and picture cues.
12 points

25. Sylvie / mettre /

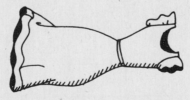

_____

26. tu / mettre /

_____

27. moi / je / ne... pas / mettre /

_____

28. nous / boire /

_____

29. je / ne... pas / boire /

_____

30. les / copains / boire /

_____

SCORE ☐

6. This part is optional. You may earn an extra ten points by writing an invitation to a party you are giving. Try to write five sentences.

_____

_____

_____

_____

_____

SCORE ☐

Test after Unit 10

1. Complete the conversations, filling in the first blank with the correct form of the verb **connaître,** and the second blank with the appropriate object pronoun.
12 points

1. —Je ne _____ pas la ville, mon vieux! —Alors, je _____ fais un plan.

2. —Nous ne _____ pas les Lardan. —Alors, je _____ présente les Lardan.

3. —Il ne _____ pas les rues. —Alors, je _____ guide.

4. —Elles ne _____ pas le parc. —Alors, je vais _____ montrer le parc.

5. —Vous ne _____ pas la résidence, vous deux? —Non, guidez-_____!

6. —Tu ne _____ pas le chemin? —Non, fais-_____ un plan, s'il te plaît.

SCORE [   ]

2. Label the floor plan of the Pierres' apartment. Use the definite article **le, la,** or **les** before each noun.
5 points

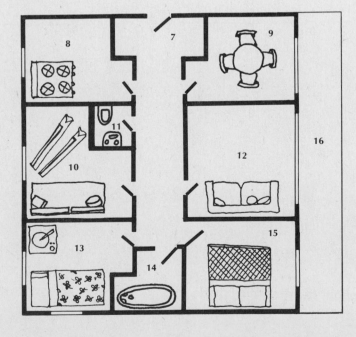

7. _____

8. _____

9. _____

10. _____

11. _____

12. _____

13. _____

14. _____

15. _____

16. _____

SCORE [   ]

3. Rewrite the sentences, replacing the underlined words with an object pronoun. Remember to make any necessary agreement of the past participle.
18 points

17. Denise a téléphoné <u>à ses amies</u>.

   _____

18. Elles ont demandé <u>à Denise</u> de jouer au tennis.

   _____

19. Denise a mis <u>sa robe de tennis</u>.

   _____

20. Elle a cherché <u>sa raquette</u>.

   _____

21. Elle a pris <u>des balles</u>.

   _____

22. Ses amies ont attendu <u>Denise</u> derrière l'école.

   _____

23. Elles ont parlé <u>à Denise</u> avant le match.

   _____

24. Les filles ont joué <u>les équipes</u> à pile ou face.

   _____

25. Denise et Anne ont gagné <u>le match</u>.

   _____

SCORE [   ]

4. Fill in the correct form of the verb **suivre.**
2½ points

26. _____-moi, s'il vous plaît.

27. Ils _____ le guide.

28. La voiture _____ la route à Dieppe.

29. Tu me _____?

30. Denis et Christine ont _____ Stéphane.

SCORE [   ]

Test after Unit 10 (continued)

5. Denis and Christine are going to Paris for the day. Write five sentences, describing their route from the Résidence Musset to the train station. Use the given words and the present tense.
10 points

sortir   tourner   suivre   croisement   à gauche   à droite   prendre   passer   devant   arriver

1	la banque	7	la gare
2	la mairie	8	la piscine
3	la poste	9	le stade
4	l'église	10	le CES
5	la Maison des Jeunes	11	la Résidence Musset
6	la pharmacie	12	les étangs

31. _____

_____

32. _____

_____

33. _____

_____

34. _____

_____

35. _____

_____

SCORE

6. Complete the sentences by matching the names of the families with the floors they live on. Write out the correct ordinal numbers.
2½ points

36. Les Chappier habitent _____.   6ᵉ les Chappier

37. Les Duclos ont un appartement _____.   5ᵉ les Caron

38. L'appartement des Dupuy est _____.   4ᵉ les Pierre

39. Les Caron sont _____.   3ᵉ les Duclos

40. Les Pierre ont acheté un appartement _____.   2ᵉ les Marchand

1ᵉʳ les Dupuy

SCORE [   ]

7. This part is optional. You may earn an extra five points by correctly identifying the places in Ville d'Avray pictured below. Use the definite article **le, la,** or **les** before each noun.

_____   _____   _____

_____   _____

SCORE [   ]

Test after Unit 11

1. Change the verbs in the following paragraph to the passé composé. Write the verb forms in the spaces provided below.
20 points

(C'est Madame Moinot qui parle.)

    Monsieur Moinot, les enfants et moi, nous allons[1] à Paris. Nous partons[2] vendredi. Quand nous y arrivons,[3] chacun va[4] de son côté. Moi, je vais[5] aux Champs-Elysées. M. Moinot, lui, va[6] au Louvre. Les enfants vont[7] à la Tour Eiffel. Moi, je reste[8] à Paris jusqu'à dimanche. M. Moinot et les enfants y restent[9] encore deux jours. Ils partent[10] mercredi.

1. _____   5. _____   8. _____

2. _____   6. _____   9. _____

3. _____   7. _____   10. _____

4. _____

SCORE [ ]

2. Fill in the passé composé of each verb in parentheses, using either **être** or **avoir.** Remember to make any necessary agreement of the past participle.
10 points

11. (passer)   Isabelle _____ une semaine à Paris.

12. (monter)   Isabelle et Antoine _____ en haut de la Tour Eiffel.

13. (sortir)   Antoine _____ son appareil-photo.

14. (descendre)   Ils _____.

15. (rentrer)   Isabelle _____ avec Antoine.

SCORE [ ]

3. Answer each question, using the pronoun **y** in your response.
5 points

16. Est-ce qu'Isabelle a passé quelques jours à Paris?

_____

17. Est-ce qu elle est restée chez son oncle et sa tante?

_____

18. Est-ce qu'Antoine et Isabelle ont fait une promenade sur la Seine?

_____

19. Est-ce qu'on peut monter en haut de la Tour Eiffel?

_____

20. Est-ce que le tombeau de Napoléon est dans l'Hôtel des Invalides?

_____

SCORE [   ]

4. Fill in the correct form of the verb **voir.**
5 points

(En haut de la Tour Eiffel, Antoine fait le guide pour un groupe de touristes.)

21. UN TOURISTE   On _____ bien d'ici! La vue est formidable!

22.   ANTOINE   Vous _____ ce bâtiment là-bas?

23. UN TOURISTE   Où? Ah oui, je le _____. Qu'est-ce que c'est?

24.   ANTOINE   C'est l'Hôtel des Invalides. On peut le _voir_ _____ encore mieux de ce côté.

25. UN TOURISTE   Moi, je l'ai déjà _____ en photo.

SCORE [   ]

Test after Unit 11 (continued)

5. Write a paragraph of five sentences describing what Isabelle and Antoine did in the picture below. Use the given words and the passé composé.
5 points

emmener — une promenade — un bateau-mouche — un pont — faire plaisir à — passer — visiter

26. _____

_____

_____

_____

_____

_____

_____

SCORE ☐

6. Choose the words that complete each sentence and write the corresponding letter in the blank.
5 points

27. _____ La Madeleine est (a) une église, (b) un hôpital, (c) un pont.

28. _____ Le Louvre est (a) une cathédrale, (b) un musée, (c) un marché.

29. _____ La Joconde est (a) à l'Hôtel des Invalides, (b) au Louvre, (c) à l'Opéra.

30. _____ Notre-Dame est (a) sur la Rive Droite, (b) sur la Rive Gauche, (c) dans l'Ile de la Cité.

31. _____ La Seine est (a) un monument, (b) un parc, (c) un fleuve.

32. _____ Dans l'Hôtel des Invalides on peut voir (a) la Joconde, (b) le tombeau de Napoléon, (c) l'Obélisque.

33. _____ Les Champs-Elysées, c'est (a) un jardin, (b) un palais, (c) une avenue.

34. _____ Le Sacré-Cœur est (a) une église, (b) un restaurant, (c) une école.

35. _____ Montmartre est (a) un quartier, (b) un fleuve, (c) un musée.

36. _____ Il y a beaucoup d'étudiants (a) dans l'Ile de la Cité, (b) dans le Quartier Latin, (c) sur les Champs-Elysées.

SCORE [   ]

7. This part is optional. You may earn an extra five points by correctly identifying the pictures. Choose from the list below.

le Louvre   Beaubourg   l'Hôtel des Invalides   le Palais de Chaillot
l'Arc de Triomphe   Notre-Dame   la Tour Eiffel   le Sacré-Cœur

_____   _____   _____

_____   _____

SCORE [   ]

Summary Test after Unit 12

1. Write out the following dates. (Do not write the year!)
5 points

1. 4/7/79 _____

2. 11/3/79 _____

3. 1/5/79 _____

4. 15/1/79 _____

5. 10/2/79 _____

SCORE ☐

2. Fill in the correct present-tense form of the verb **écrire**.
5 points

6. A qui est-ce que tu _____?

7. J'_____ à ma grand-mère.

8. Jean-Marcel _____ à ses cousins.

9. Ses cousins n'_____ jamais.

10. Est-ce que vous _____ une lettre?

SCORE ☐

3. Rewrite the sentences, changing the verb to the passé composé. Use either **avoir** or **être,** and make any necessary agreement of the past participle.
20 points

EXAMPLES: Nous la trouvons.   *Nous l'avons trouvée.*

Ils y vont.   *Ils y sont allés.*

11. Elle y entre.

_____

12. Vous la voyez?

_____

13. Tu en prends?

_____

14. Nous y restons.

_____

15. J'en bois.

_____

16. Nous leur écrivons.

_____

17. Elle la perd.

_____

18. Ils nous suivent, mon frère et moi!

_____

19. Elles en sortent.

_____

20. Il la met.

_____

SCORE ☐

Summary Test after Unit 12 (continued)

4. Answer the following questions as if you were Jean-Marcel Giuliani. Write complete sentences, using the appropriate object pronoun: **le, la, les, lui, leur, y,** or **en.**
20 points

21. Vous et vos parents, vous êtes allés à Monaco?

_____

22. Vous avez rencontré le Prince?

_____

_____

23. Vous avez visité le Musée Océanographique?

_____

24. Il faut acheter des billets pour entrer?

_____

25. Vous avez vu les soucoupes plongeantes?

_____

26. Vous êtes descendus à l'aquarium?

_____

27. Vous êtes montés à la terrasse?

_____

28. Vous avez visité la salle de zoologie?

_____

29. Votre père a pris des photos?

_____

30. Vous avez écrit à vos cousins?

_____

SCORE [   ]

5. Rewrite the sentences, replacing the underlined word with a word which is opposite in meaning. The new word must fit the sentence grammatically.
10 points

31. Les touristes sont <u>montés</u>.

_____

32. La voiture est <u>derrière</u> la gare.

_____

33. Je vais <u>vendre</u> le télescope.

_____

34. La surprise-partie a <u>commencé</u>.

_____

35. Vous <u>économisez</u> tout votre argent.

_____

36. Sylvie aime mieux les danses <u>rapides</u>.

_____

37. Le bateau-mouche <u>arrive</u>.

_____

38. Nous avons tourné à <u>droite</u>.

_____

39. Il est <u>blanc</u>.

_____

40. François est <u>entré</u>.

_____

SCORE ☐

Summary Test after Unit 12 (continued)

6. Write five vocabulary words under each heading below.
10 points

LES VETEMENTS

41. _____

42. _____

43. _____

44. _____

45. _____

LES BATIMENTS

51. _____

52. _____

53. _____

54. _____

55. _____

LA FAMILLE

46. _____

47. _____

48. _____

49. _____

50. _____

LES PROFESSIONS

56. _____

57. _____

58. _____

59. _____

60. _____

SCORE [   ]

7. Rewrite the sentences as if you were talking to an adult who is not a member of your family.
5 points

61. Tu me connais? _____

62. Je t'attends ici. _____

63. Je viens avec toi. _____

64. Tu m'entends? _____

65. Décris ton appartement. _____

SCORE [   ]

8. Pretend that you are Jean-Marcel Giuliani. You are spending some time with Denis and Christine Pierre, who have an apartment in the Résidence Musset in Ville d'Avray, a suburb of Paris. Write a letter of at least ten sentences to your parents in Nice, telling them about (a) the Pierres, (b) their apartment, (c) Ville d'Avray, (d) an excursion to Paris with Denis and Christine, (e) other activities that you enjoyed. Write an appropriate opening and closing to your letter.
25 points

_____ , _____

_____ ,

_____

_____

_____

_____

_____

SCORE [ ]

Test after Unit 13

1. Complete each sentence by choosing an appropriate reflexive verb from the list below and writing its correct form in the blank.
10 points

s'arrêter	s'habiller	se lever
se dépêcher	se coucher	se brosser
se promener	se maquiller	se reposer
se rendre		

1. Marianne _____. Elle met une jupe et un chemisier.

2. L'autobus _____ devant le magasin.

3. Il fait beau! Je vais _____ dans le parc.

4. Michel! Sylvie! _____! Il est déjà sept heures!

5. Je me lave et puis je _____.

6. Est-ce que vous _____ avant minuit?

7. Tu as l'air épuisé! _____ un peu!

8. Nous _____ les cheveux.

9. Comment est-ce que tu _____ à ton travail? En autobus?

10. Quand mon réveil sonne, je _____ d'un bond!   SCORE ☐

2. Identify the following toilet articles. Use an article before the noun to indicate the gender of the word.
5 points

11.

_____

12.

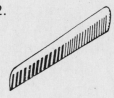

_____

13.

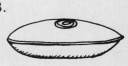

_____

14.

_____

15.

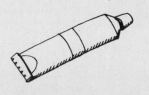

_____

SCORE ☐

3. Complete the sentences by choosing the appropriate verb and writing its correct form in the blank.
10 points

16. Nous _____ le chien. (promener, se promener)

17. Viviane _____ à sept heures. (réveiller, se réveiller)

18. M. Lardan _____ la voiture. (laver, se laver)

19. Vous _____ dans le jardin? (promener, se promener)

20. Le matin, François _____ les mains. (laver, se laver)

21. Les jeunes _____ à la surprise-partie. (amuser, s'amuser)

22. Maman _____ les enfants. (réveiller, se réveiller)

23. Je _____ après mon travail. (reposer, se reposer)

24. Oncle Jules _____ les enfants. (amuser, s'amuser)

25. Tu ne _____ pas ta bague? (trouver, se trouver)

SCORE ☐

4. Rewrite the sentences in the negative, using **ne** and either **rien** or **personne.**
10 points

26. Vous prenez quelque chose? _____

27. Je connais quelqu'un. _____

28. Quelqu'un répond. _____

29. Tu entends quelque chose? _____

30. Quelque chose a changé. _____

31. Je vois quelqu'un. _____

32. Elle a acheté quelque chose. _____

33. Nous avons vu quelqu'un. _____

34. Il va emmener quelqu'un. _____

35. Elle veut manger quelque chose. _____

SCORE ☐

Test after Unit 13 (continued)

5. Describe Viviane's typical day, expanding the following composition. For each topic sentence given, write two additional sentences that continue the thought.
15 points

36. Viviane se lève à sept heures. _____

_____

_____

37. Elle se rend à son travail. _____

_____

_____

38. A midi elle déjeune. _____

_____

_____

39. L'après-midi de Viviane n'est pas très différent de sa matinée. _____

_____

_____

40. A sept heures et demie elle arrive chez elle. _____

_____

_____

SCORE [   ]

6. This part is optional. You may earn an extra ten points by completing the sentences with words from the list below.

tartine   magasin   exposition   client   affluence
trajet   vaisselle   patron   bol   cravate

1. Viviane travaille dans un _____.

2. Quelqu'un qui achète quelque chose est un _____.

3. Quand tout le monde rentre après son travail, c'est l'heure d'_____.

4. Après le dîner Viviane fait la _____.

5. On va au musée pour voir une _____.

6. M. Simorre a un rendez-vous important. Il met une chemise et une _____.

7. L'homme pour qui on travaille est un _____.

8. Elle ne peut pas y aller à pied! C'est un long _____!

9. Le matin, Viviane prend un _____ de chocolat et une _____.

SCORE _____

Test after Unit 14

1. Write sentences, telling which instrument each person plays.
7 points

1. Bernard

2. Olivier

3. Didier

4. Jean-Marie

5. Philippe

6. Catherine

7. Bruno

1. _____

2. _____

3. _____

4. _____

5. _____

6. _____

7. _____

SCORE ☐

2. Write sentences in the present tense, using the given words and picture cues.
   8 points

   8. Olivier / préférer /

   _____

   9. je / préférer /

   _____

   10. nous / préférer /

   _____

   11. camarades / préférer /

   _____

SCORE [ ]

3. Use **venir de** + *infinitive* to answer each question, stating that the action has just happened.
   10 points

   12. Est-ce que tu as téléphoné?

   Oui, _____

   13. Est-ce que Bernard est descendu?

   Oui, _____

   14. Les membres du groupe ont répété?

   Oui, _____

   15. La répétition a commencé?

   Oui, _____

   16. Est-ce que vous avez chanté, vous et Philippe?

   Oui, _____

     SCORE [ ]

Test after Unit 14 (continued)

4. Write a complete question for each statement, using the correct form of the interrogative adjective **(quel, etc.).** Make any necessary agreement of the past participle.
10 points

EXAMPLE: J'ai aimé cette chanson.

Quelle chanson est-ce que tu as aimée?

17. Catherine a apporté le magnétophone.

_____

18. J'ai enregistré cet air.

_____

19. Ils ont joué plusieurs morceaux.

_____

20. Elle a écrit ces compositions.

_____

21. Nous avons perdu la bande!

_____

SCORE [   ]

5. Complete the conversations, filling in the first blank with the correct interrogative pronoun **(lequel, etc.)** and the second blank with the correct demonstrative pronoun **(celui, etc.).**
10 points

EXAMPLE: —Montrez-moi ce banjo, s'il vous plaît.

—_____ *Lequel* _____ ?

—_____ *Celui* _____ -là.

22. —Tu as aimé les chansons?   23. —Mettez cette bande.

—_____ ?   —_____ ?

—_____ du chanteur   —_____ -là.
américain.

24. —Vérifiez les haut-parleurs.

—_____?

—_____-la.

25. —Un des micros ne marche pas!

—_____?

—_____ à droite.

26. —Ils sont allés à une kermesse.

—A _____?

—A _____ de Luneray.

SCORE [   ]

6. Write a vocabulary word that fits the given definition. Use an article before each noun.
5 points

27. Un genre de musique: _____

28. Une saison: _____

29. Quelqu'un qui chante: _____

30. Quelqu'un qui joue de la musique: _____

31. Quelqu'un qui joue du piano: _____

SCORE [   ]

7. This part is optional. You may earn an extra ten points. Write an imaginary conversation between yourself and a friend about a tape recorder that you have just bought. All of the statements or questions you write need not be complete sentences.

Vous _____

Votre Ami(e) _____

Vous _____

Votre Ami(e) _____

Vous _____

SCORE [   ]

Test after Unit 15

1. Rewrite the sentences, changing the verb to the passé composé. Make any necessary agreement of the past participle.
20 points

1. Les skieurs se réchauffent autour du feu.

   _____

2. Je me prépare du chocolat.

   _____

3. Louise s'appuie sur le bras de Denise.

   _____

4. Denise se relève après l'accident.

   _____

5. Louise se réchauffe les mains.

   _____

6. La monitrice se casse la jambe.

   _____

7. Je me fais mal.

   _____

8. Est-ce que tu te couches de bonne heure, Jocelyne?

   _____

9. Les filles s'élancent avant nous.

   _____

10. Nous nous achetons des lunettes.

    _____

SCORE [   ]

2. Write two sentences for each picture: tell what season it is and describe the weather.
8 points

11. 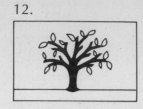　12. 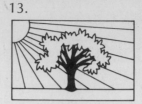　13. 　14.

11. _____

_____

12. _____

_____

13. _____

_____

14. _____

_____

SCORE ☐

3. List the items (ski equipment and clothing) shown in the picture. Use the indefinite article **un, une,** or **des.**
7 points

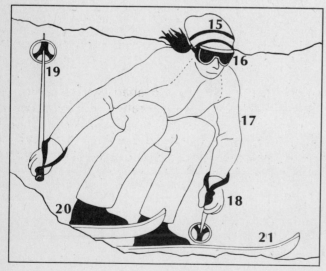

15. _____

16. _____

17. _____

18. _____

19. _____

20. _____

21. _____

SCORE ☐

Test after Unit 16

1. Fill in the correct present-tense form of either **savoir** or **connaître.**
5 points

1. Je ne _____ pas cette région.

2. Est-ce que vous _____ où ils sont allés?

3. Mon oncle est très intelligent! Il _____ tout!

4. Les cousins _____ conduire le tracteur.

5. Nous _____ les parents de Georgette.

SCORE [   ]

2. Write sentences in the present tense, using the given words and picture cues. Add any necessary articles and make the adjective agree with the noun.
10 points

6. fermier/vendre/vieux/

_____

7. sur/étang/nous/voir/beau/

_____

8. ce/être/vieux/

_____

9. nous/avoir/nouveau/

_____

10. beau/abriter/maison

3. Write sentences, telling what each person is doing. Use the present tense of the verb.
10 points

11. Alain 12. Georgette 13. Louis et Angel 14. Monique 15. Jean-François

11. _____

12. _____

13. _____

14. _____

15. _____

4. Replace the infinitives in the following paragraph with the correct imparfait form of the verb. Write the verb forms in the spaces provided below.
10 points

Je (passer[16]) mes vacances dans la ferme de mon oncle. La journée (commencer[17]) très tôt. Nous (se lever[18]) à cinq heures! Mon oncle Guy (s'occuper[19]) des vaches, et j'(aider[20]) Jean-Pierre. Mon cousin Jean-Pierre (avoir[21]) dix-sept ans. Il (savoir[22]) conduire le tracteur. Ma cousine et ma tante (faire[23]) de la confiture. Quelquefois elles (aller[24]) travailler aux champs. Nous (être[25]) tous très occupés!

16. _____ 19. _____ 22. _____ 24. _____

17. _____ 20. _____ 23. _____ 25. _____

18. _____ 21. _____

Test after Unit 16 (continued)

5. Fill in the missing words.
5 points

blé	mûres	étable	hangar	plante
mur	noisettes	grange	foin	cheval

26. Il nous laissait monter son _____.

27. On met le _____ dans le grenier.

28. Au printemps on _____ le jardin.

29. Dans la ferme il y a des champs de _____.

30. Le fermier met le tracteur dans le _____.

31. Mme Fort fait de la confiture avec les _____.

32. Quand il fait froid les vaches restent dans l' _____.

33. En automne on va cueillir les _____ dans le bois.

34. On trouve des animaux et de l'équipement dans la _____.

35. Les animaux ne sortent pas; il y a un _____ autour de la ferme.

SCORE [   ]

6. Imagine that you used to live in the village of Ore when you were younger. Referring to the picture post card below, write five sentences describing Ore as you remember it. All the verbs must be in the imparfait.
10 points

Souvenirs d'Ore

36. _____

_____

37. _____

_____

38. _____

_____

39. _____

_____

40. _____

_____

SCORE ☐

Test after Unit 17

1. Rewrite the sentences, adding the correct form of the verb in parentheses and making any other necessary changes.
10 points
EXAMPLE: Je me couche. (aller)

Je vais me coucher.

1. Nous explorons la forêt. (vouloir)

_____

2. Tu répares l'électrophone? (pouvoir)

_____   _____

3. Les Fort visitent les Antilles. (vouloir)

_____

4. Nous attendons ici. (pouvoir)

_____

5. Tu ne finis pas ta langouste? (vouloir)

_____

6. Louise achète les timbres. (pouvoir)

_____

7. Est-ce que vous prenez un taxi? (vouloir)

_____

8. Je vous montre le chemin. (pouvoir)

_____

9. Ils pêchent dans la baie. (pouvoir)

_____

10. M. Daquin vend son vieux bateau. (vouloir)

_____

SCORE ☐

2. Change the verbs in the following paragraph to the appropriate past tense, either the imparfait or the passé composé. Write the verb forms in the spaces provided below.
15 points

   Aujourd'hui Doris et Danou décident[11] d'aller à la plage. Quand ils y arrivent,[12] il fait[13] bon. Un vent doux vient[14] de l'ouest. Des gens se bronzent[15] au soleil. Doris se baigne[16] pendant deux heures! Danou cherche[17] des coquillages exotiques. Il se promène[18] sur la plage quand il entend[19] quelqu'un dans l'eau. C'est[20] un homme qui ne peut[21] plus nager! Il est[22] épuisé; il a[23] mal à la jambe! Danou plonge[24] dans la mer et ramène[25] l'homme sur la plage!

11. _____   16. _____   21. _____

12. _____   17. _____   22. _____

13. _____   18. _____   23. _____

14. _____   19. _____   24. _____

15. _____   20. _____   25. _____

SCORE [____]

3. List the items that Danou is wearing and carrying in the picture. Use the article **un, une,** or **des.**
5 points

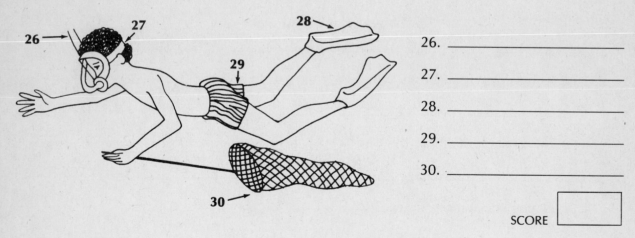

26. _____

27. _____

28. _____

29. _____

30. _____

SCORE [____]

Test after Unit 17 (continued)

4. Write six sentences about Martinique. Tell what it is. Give its location. Identify the capital city. Tell what the land is like. Describe the climate. Tell what language is spoken there.
12 points

31. _____

32. _____

33. _____

34. _____

_____

35. _____

36. _____

SCORE [   ]

5. In the space provided on the left, write the word or phrase that has the same meaning as the underlined word or phrase in the sentence. What you write must fit the sentence grammatically.
8 points

37. _____   Nous allons <u>à la plage</u>.

38. _____   Je vais <u>attraper des poissons</u>.

39. _____   Daquin est un <u>homme qui attrape des poissons</u>.

40. _____ Une très grande vague a jeté Danou sur le rocher.

41. _____ Notre bateau est passé près d'un grand rocher dans l'eau!

42. _____ Mme Dubois est une femme qui aide les familles qui ont des difficultés.

43. _____ C'est le lieu du débarquement de Christophe Colomb.

44. _____ Cousteau a fait des explorations sous l'eau.

SCORE [   ]

6. This part is optional. You may earn an extra eight points. Referring to the map of Martinique, complete each sentence by telling how many kilometers the first city is to the north, south, east, or west of the second city. Then translate the kilometers into miles. Remember that 1 km = 0.62 mi.

DISCARD

EXAMPLE: Sainte-Marie est à ___7___ kilomètres *au sud* de Marigot. Ça fait ___4,34___ miles.

1. Fort-de-France est à _____ kilomètres

    _____ de Case-Pilote. Ça fait

    _____ miles.

2. Grand'Rivière est à _____ kilomètres

    _____ de Basse-Pointe. Ça fait

    _____ miles.

3. Saint-Pierre est à _____ kilomètres

    _____ du Carbet. Ça fait

    _____ miles.

4. Le François est à _____ kilomètres

    _____ de Fort-de-France. Ça fait

    _____ miles.

SCORE [   ]

Summary Test after Unit 18

1. Fill in the present tense of the verb in parentheses.
10 points

    1. (venir)   Nous _____ tous les ans.

    2. (vouloir)   Est-ce que tu _____ voir le bateau?

    3. (savoir)   Est-ce que tu _____ faire de la voile?

    4. (pouvoir)   François ne _____ pas s'endormir.

    5. (savoir)   Mes amis ne _____ pas l'alphabet Morse.

    6. (venir)   Les vipères ne _____ pas près du camp.

    7. (pouvoir)   Est-ce que vous _____ déchiffrer ce message?

    8. (vouloir)   Les garçons de l'autre équipe ne _____ pas faire la veille!

    9. (venir)   Est-ce que tu _____ au lac avec nous?

    10. (savoir)   Le chef _____ faire les nœuds.

SCORE ☐

2. Imagine that you are up in the watchtower at the sailing camp, looking out over the lake. Your friend is shouting up to you. Complete the following conversation, filling in the correct form of the words in parentheses.
6 points

    L'AMI   Il y a quelqu'un sur ces rochers là-bas?

    11. VOUS   _____ rochers? (quel)

    12. L'AMI   _____ à droite. (celui)

    VOUS   Oui, c'est une fille qui se bronze.

    L'AMI   Regarde cette voile là-bas!

    13. VOUS   _____? (lequel)

    14. L'AMI   _____ près des rochers. (celui)

    VOUS   Ce n'est pas une voile! C'est un oiseau!

    L'AMI   Regarde! Il y a quelqu'un perché dans ce pin!

15. VOUS _____? (lequel)

16. L'AMI _____ derrière la tente. (celui)

   VOUS   Ce n'est pas une personne! C'est un animal!

3. Fill in the present tense of the verb in parentheses.
   10 points

17. (se bronzer)   Sylvie _____ au soleil.

18. (s'installer)   Les skieurs _____ près du feu.

19. (se réunir)   Nous _____ pour notre leçon.

20. (se détendre)   Après une longue journée de ski, je _____.

21. (se promener)   Ils _____ dans les bois.

22. (se charger)   C'est toi qui _____ des bateaux?

23. (s'habiller)   Je _____ avant le petit déjeuner.

24. (se souvenir)   Est-ce que vous _____ de l'excursion?

25. (se maquiller)   Ma sœur ne _____ jamais.

26. (s'amuser)   Est-ce que tu _____?

Summary Test after Unit 18 (continued)

4. Fill in the passé composé of the verb in parentheses. Remember to make any necessary agreement of the past participle.
   20 points

27. (se laver)   Nous _____ les dents.

28. (se brosser)   Elle _____ les cheveux.

29. (se lever)   Ils _____ avant le soleil.

30. (se coucher)   Je _____ dans mon sac de couchage.

31. (se promener)   Elles _____ dans les dunes.

32. (s'installer)   Nous _____ sous les pins.

33. (se changer)   Viviane _____ dans la tente.

34. (se laver)   Vous _____ à la pompe, vous deux?

35. (se dépêcher)   Pourquoi est-ce que tu _____?

36. (s'occuper)   François _____ de la vaisselle.

SCORE _____

5. Choose the word that is *not* related to the others and write its letter in the blank.
   4 points

37. _____   (a) l'été   (b) l'hiver   (c) le pré   (d) l'automne

38. _____   (a) une baie   (b) un champ   (c) un lac   (d) un étang

39. _____   (a) le bras   (b) la vitrine   (c) le genou   (d) la jambe

40. _____   (a) la poule   (b) la paille   (c) le cochon   (d) le canard

SCORE _____

6. Rewrite the sentences, putting the adjective in its correct form and place.
10 points

41. La pompe ne marchait pas. (vieux)

_____

42. Qui est dans la tente? (voisin)

_____

43. On se trouvait sur un lac. (beau)

_____

44. Nous avons plongé dans l'eau. (clair)

_____

45. Il y avait deux dunes près du camp. (énorme)

_____

46. Regardez les pins! (beau)

_____

47. J'aime beaucoup ces couleurs. (brillant)

_____

48. Ils ont acheté une voile. (nouveau)

_____

49. A Saint-Sauveur j'ai fait la connaissance d'une monitrice. (canadien)

_____

_____

50. De notre chambre nous avons une vue. (impressionant)

_____

SCORE [   ]

Summary Test after Unit 18 (continued)

7. Fill in either the imparfait or the passé composé of the verb in parentheses.
20 points

51. Ce jour-là les musiciens ont répété jusqu'à cinq heures, mais en général ils

    _____ à quatre heures. (finir)

52. Cet été nous sommes allés dans une école de voile, mais en général nous

    _____ l'été dans une ferme. (passer)

53. En général Viviane déjeune seule, mais hier elle _____ une amie.
    (rencontrer)

54. Aujourd'hui Saint-Pierre est un petit village, mais autrefois c'_____ une
    ville importante. (être)

55. En général il jouait du piano, mais ce jour-là il _____ Philippe au
    saxophone. (remplacer)

56. En général elle portait un jean, mais ce jour-là elle _____ une jupe.
    (mettre)

57. Ce jour-là vous êtes tombé, mais en général vous _____ sans difficulté.
    (descendre)

58. En général il ne neigeait pas beaucoup, mais cet hiver-là nous _____
    plusieurs tempêtes de neige. (avoir)

59. Ils prenaient toujours la piste pour les novices, mais cette fois-là ils _____
    celle pour les intermédiaires. (choisir)

60. Cette année il a planté du maïs dans ce champs, mais autrefois il y _____
    du blé. (cultiver)

SCORE [   ]

8. Imagine that you are old. You are reminiscing about the sailing camp where you *used to* spend your summers. Tell what it was like, what you used to do. Then, relate an outstanding incident that *happened once* involving a snake. Write in the past tense and make correct use of the imparfait and the passé composé. Write ten sentences.
20 points

Tous les ans, je _____

_____

_____

_____

_____

_____

_____

_____

_____

_____

_____

_____

_____

_____

_____

_____

_____

_____

_____

SCORE [ ]

Test after Unit 19

1. Fill in the correct present-tense form of the verb **dire**.
6 points

1. Qu'est-ce que vous _____?

2. Elle est très timide. Elle ne _____ rien.

3. Ecoute ce que je te _____!

4. Mes parents _____ toujours ça!

5. Pourquoi est-ce que tu _____ ça?

6. Vous comprenez ce que nous _____?

SCORE _____

2. Combine each pair of sentences into one, using the reflexive form of the verb.
12 points
EXAMPLE: Richard a vu Nigel. Nigel a vu Richard.
_____ *Ils se sont vus.* _____

7. Marie aime Pierre. Pierre aime Marie.

_____

8. Marie a reconnu François. François á reconnu Marie.

_____

9. Jacques ressemble à Paul. Paul ressemble à Jacques.

_____

10. Philippe a rencontré Yvonne. Yvonne a rencontré Philippe.

_____

SCORE _____

3. Fill in the blanks, telling where each person lives and what language he or she speaks.
12 points

EXAMPLE: C'est une Française. Elle habite _____ *en France* _____. Elle parle _____ *français* _____.

11. C'est un Anglais.

    Il habite _____.

    Il parle _____.

12. C'est une Espagnole.

    Elle habite _____.

    Elle parle _____.

13. C'est un Marocain.

    Il habite _____.

    Il parle _____.

14. C'est un Allemand.

    Il habite _____.

    Il parle _____.

15. C'est un Russe.

    Il habite _____.

    Il parle _____.

16. C'est une Italienne.

    Elle habite _____.

    Elle parle _____.

SCORE ☐

Test after Unit 19 (continued)

4. Referring to the "Tableau des Arrivées," write sentences that tell from which country each flight is arriving and at what time. Translate official time into unofficial time.
10 points

EXAMPLE: *Le vol 606 arrive de Turquie à trois heures et demie.*

	ARRIVEES	
Vol	*Provenance*	*Horaire*
AF 606	Ankara	15:30
AF 304	Dakar	16:05
TW 801	New York	15:00
AF 138	Tel Aviv	15:15
AA 18	Rabat	17:00
AF 607	Bruxelles	17:30

17. _____

_____

18. _____

_____

19. _____

_____

20. _____

_____

21. _____

_____

SCORE _____

5. Fill in the missing words. Use the vocabulary relating to an airplane flight that you have learned in this chapter. The words must fit the sentence grammatically.
10 points

Nous avons acheté nos _____ une semaine avant notre départ. Le jour de

notre départ nous sommes allés en taxi à _____ Charles de Gaulle. Nous

allions prendre le _____ Air France 801, _____ à 16 h

en Israël. Nous sommes montés dans un grand _____; c'était un Boeing

747. Notre 747 a _____ à l'heure. Une jolie _____

nous a _____ d'attacher nos ceintures. Après quelques heures, nous avons

_____ à Tel Aviv. Nous sommes arrivés avec une heure de retard à cause

du _____.

SCORE [   ]

6. This part is optional. You may earn an extra ten points. Write a conversation you might have with a passenger sitting next to you on the airplane. Try to write ten lines.

VOUS _____

LE (LA) PASSAGER(ERE) _____

_____

_____

_____

_____

_____

_____

_____

_____

_____

_____

SCORE [   ]

Test after Unit 20

1. Rewrite the sentences, adding the correct form of the verb in parentheses, plus the preposition **à** or **de** if necessary. Make other necessary changes.
20 points
EXAMPLE: (commencer) Nadia prépare le couscous.

$\qquad$ *Nadia commence à préparer le couscous.*
_____

1. (apprendre) Je joue aux échecs.

_____

2. (décider) Nous pique-niquons à la plage.

_____

3. (finir) Les musiciens répètent.

_____

4. (continuer) Il raconte ses aventures.

_____

5. (aimer) Est-ce que vous marchandez?

_____

6. (avoir envie) Est-ce que tu flânes dans les souks?

_____

7. (aider) Catherine a rangé la pièce.

_____

8. (préférer) Tu restes à la maison?

_____

9. (vouloir) Elle a mis son collier.

_____

10. (s'amuser) Les enfants regardent les animaux.

_____

SCORE [   ]

2. Write two sentences about each picture: identify the craftsperson, and tell what he or she makes.
10 points

EXAMPLE:

C'est un boulanger.
Il fait du pain.

11.   12.   13.

14.   15.

11. _____

_____

12. _____

_____

13. _____

_____

14. _____

_____

15. _____

_____

SCORE

Test after Unit 20 (continued)

3. Complete the question with the correct interrogative pronoun suggested by the answer: **qui est-ce qui, qui est-ce que, qu'est-ce qui, qu'est-ce que, qui,** or **quoi.**
   12 points

   EXAMPLE: —___*Qui (est-ce qui)*___ vient d'arriver? —Armand.

   16. —A _____ est-ce qu'ils jouent? —Aux boules.

   17. —Pour _____ est-ce que Samir achète le portefeuille? —Pour son père.

   18. —_____ ils attendent? —M. Slim.

   19. _____ Mme Slim prépare? —Un couscous.

   20. —_____ a fait la salade méchouia? —C'est Leïla qui l'a faite.

   21. —_____ a cassé la vitrine? —Un rocher.

   SCORE [   ]

4. Describe the picture by filling in the missing words.
   2 points

22. Ce soir, les Slim ont des _____ chez eux.

23. Après le dîner, ils vont au _____.

24. Là, ils prennent le _____.

25. Mme Slim le sert dans un _____, pas dans une tasse.

SCORE [   ]

5. What do the pictures show about Tunisian life and customs? Write one sentence for each picture.
6 points

26.  27.  28.

26. _____

_____

27. _____

_____

28. _____

_____

SCORE ☐

Test after Unit 21

1. Rewrite each sentence two different ways: (a) using **après** + *past infinitive* (to state that someone did one thing *after having completed* the other); (b) using **avant de** (to state that someone did one thing *before doing* the other).
10 points
EXAMPLE: Nous dînons, et puis nous sortons.

Après avoir dîné, nous sommes sortis.

Nous avons dîné avant de sortir.

1. Les élèves jouent à cache-cache, et puis ils retournent en classe.

   _____

   _____

   _____

2. J'écris des lettres, et puis je me couche.

   _____

   _____

3. Sylvie se lave, et puis elle s'habille.

   _____

   _____

4. Nous épluchons les légumes, et puis nous mettons la table.

   _____

   _____

5. Samir marchande un peu, et puis il achète le portefeuille.

   _____

   _____

SCORE [   ]

2. Rewrite the following paragraph, changing the **aller** + *infinitive* verb forms to the future tense. For example: **vous allez sortir** becomes **vous sortirez.**
20 points

6.   Pour nos vacances, voici ce que nous allons faire l'année prochaine: nous allons aller en Angleterre. Papa va louer une voiture, comme ça nous allons pouvoir visiter le pays sans difficultés. Ma sœur va rencontrer sa correspondante anglaise pour la première fois. Mon frère va avoir l'occasion de visiter la Tour de Londres, son rêve depuis longtemps. Ma mère va s'acheter des pulls. Moi, je vais apporter mon appareil et vais prendre des tas de photos. Je suis sûr que nous allons être très contents de notre séjour.

SCORE

Test after Unit 21 (continued)

3. Referring to the pictures below, describe Anna's and Sylvie's day at the "fête foraine." Write one sentence for each picture, using the past tense and varying your sentences so that you do not use the same verb each time.
14 points

7. Le samedi, Anna et Sylvie sont allées à la fête foraine. _____

_____

_____

_____

_____

_____

_____

_____

_____

SCORE

4. Combine each pair of sentences into one, using the preposition in parentheses + an infinitive.
6 points

EXAMPLE: Elle a téléphoné. Elle nous a invités à dîner. (pour)

Elle a téléphoné pour nous inviter à dîner.

8. Il est parti. Il n'a pas dit au revoir. (sans)

_____

9. Ils sont descendus. Ils ne sont pas tombés. (sans)

_____

10. Nous vendons des légumes de notre jardin. Nous gagnons un peu d'argent. (pour)

_____

_____

11. J'ai apporté le magnétophone. J'ai enregistré le concert. (pour)

_____

12. Je me suis couché. Je ne me suis pas déshabillé. (sans)

_____

13. Nous nous sommes arrêtés. Nous avons admiré la vue. (pour)

_____

SCORE [   ]

5. This part is optional. You may earn an extra six points. Imagine that you are conversing with your friend at the "fête foraine." Choose your responses from the list below.

—Comment ça marche?　　　—Non, j'ai le vertige.
—Tiens-toi bien!　　　　　—Froussard(e)!
—Ça me suffit!　　　　　　—C'est extra!

1. —Encore un tour sur le grand huit? —_____

2. —Tu as le mal de mer? —_____ _____

3. —Tu veux essayer cette machine? —_____

4. —Comment trouves-tu la maison magique? —_____

5. —Moi, j'ai peur! —_____

6. —Je vais tomber! —_____

SCORE [   ]

Test after Unit 22

1. Combine each pair of sentences into one, replacing the adjective with the corresponding adverb.
5 points
EXAMPLE: Pierre étudie. Il est distrait.

Pierre étudie distraitement.

1. Louis est le champion. C'est indiscutable!

_____

2. Guy fait les exercices. Il est lent.

_____

3. Notre équipe est la meilleure. C'est certain!

_____

4. M. Lefort dirige l'entraînement. Il est sérieux.

_____

5. Hélène est douée en gymnastique. C'est vrai!

_____

SCORE ☐

2. Fill in the correct form and tense of the verb **courir.**
5 points

6. Aujourd'hui je _____ le 100 m et François _____ le 800 m.

7. Samedi dernier Suzanne _____ les haies.

8. Les athlètes ne _____ pas la semaine prochaine.

9. Quand M. Lefort, le professeur de gymnastique, était jeune, il _____ le 800 m.

SCORE ☐

3. Combine each pair of sentences into one, making a statement of comparison by using an appropriate adjective or adverb.
12 points

EXAMPLE: Denise a 12 ans. Doris a 13 ans. _Denise est plus jeune que Doris._

10. Suzanne mesure 1,57 m. Sa sœur mesure 1,62 m.

_____

11. Philippe a 12 en maths. Georges a 9 en maths.

_____

_____

12. Suzanne saute 1,22 m. Jean-François saute 1,73 m.

_____

13. Louis lance le poids à 12 m. Paul le lance à 13 m.

_____

_____

14. A la course le temps d'Hélène est de 13″4. Celui de Viviane est de 13″4.

_____

15. Les pommes de terre coûtent 1 F le kilo. Les carottes coûtent 1 F le kilo.

_____

_____

SCORE [ ]

4. Write a sentence with the superlative, stating that the *underlined* person is best.
8 points

EXAMPLE: Denise et <u>Catherine</u> sont intelligentes. _Catherine est la plus intelligente._

16. Marie, Suzanne, Viviane et <u>Louise</u> jouent bien au tennis.

_____

17. <u>Paul</u>, François et Philippe sont bons en géographie.

_____

Test after Unit 22 (continued)

18. Louis, Jean-François et <u>Hélène</u> sont distraits à l'entraînement.

_____

19. Raymond, <u>Ghislaine</u> et Yves nagent rapidement.

_____

SCORE ☐

5. List the parts of the body indicated in the picture. Use the definite article **le** or **la**.
10 points

20. _____   27. _____   34. _____

21. _____   28. _____   35. _____

22. _____   29. _____   36. _____

23. _____   30. _____   37. _____

24. _____   31. _____   38. _____

25. _____   32. _____   39. _____

26. _____   33. _____

SCORE ☐

6. Write five sentences in the past tense about an imaginary race that you ran yesterday. Use the given words.
10 points

participer — les concurrents — le favori/la favorite — courir — remporter

40. _____

41. _____

42. _____

43. _____

44. _____

SCORE [____]

7. This part is optional. You may earn an extra five points by listing the equipment pictured in the gymnasium below. Use the definite article **le, la,** or **les.**

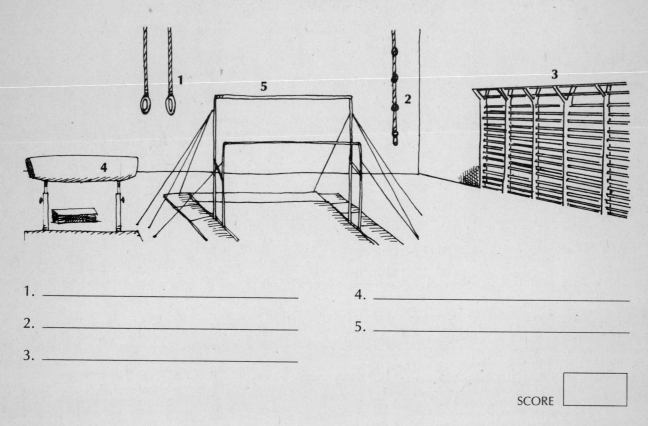

1. _____   4. _____

2. _____   5. _____

3. _____

SCORE [____]

Test after Unit 23

1. Fill in the correct possessive pronoun: **le mien, etc.**
6 points

1. J'ai oublié ma carte. Tu as _____?

2. Nous avons acheté notre voiture à Paris. Où est-ce que vous avez acheté

   _____?

3. Anna a lu son horoscope, mais Sylvie n'a pas voulu lire _____.

4. Doris range toujours sa chambre, mais ses frères ne rangent jamais _____.

5. J'ai dû emprunter des skis à mon frère. _____ sont cassés.

6. Philippe a prêté sa montre à Vincent. Vincent a perdu _____.

SCORE _____

2. Rewrite the sentences, expressing a real possibility.
10 points

EXAMPLE: Je n'ai pas d'argent parce que je ne fais pas d'économies.
   Si je fais des économies, j'aurai de l'argent.

7. François n'a pas de bonnes notes parce qu'il n'étudie pas.

   _____

8. Vous ne comprenez pas parce que vous ne faites pas attention.

   _____

9. Tu n'apprends pas parce que tu n'es pas sérieux.

   _____

10. Nous ne savons pas les réponses parce que nous ne finissons pas nos devoirs.

    _____

11. Elle ne répond pas bien aux questions parce qu'elle n'écoute pas le professeur.

    _____

SCORE _____

3. Rewrite each pair of statements of fact as one conditional sentence expressing an impossibility.
12 points

EXAMPLE: Je n'ai pas assez d'argent. Je n'achète pas le cadeau.

Si j'avais assez d'argent, j'achèterais le cadeau.

12. Tu ne vas pas dans les souks. Tu ne vois pas les artisans.

_____

13. Le magnétophone ne marche pas. Nous n'enregistrons pas la musique.

_____

14. Elle n'a pas le reçu. Elle n'échange pas les gants.

_____

15. Ils n'achètent pas les sandales. Ils ne connaissent pas sa taille.

_____

16. Vous n'êtes pas en forme. Vous ne faites pas d'exercices.

_____

17. Il n'y a pas de papier à lettres. Je n'écris pas un petit mot.

_____

SCORE ☐

4. Using the given words and picture cues, write a sentence in the passé composé telling where the person bought the gift.
12 points

18. Vincent/acheter/

_____

_____

19. Xavier/acheter/

_____

_____

Test after Unit 23 (continued)

20. Vincent et Françoise/acheter/

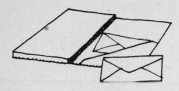

_____

_____

_____

21. Françoise/acheter/

_____

_____

22. Maman/acheter/

_____

_____

23. Frédérique/acheter/

_____

_____

SCORE [ ]

5. Write a paragraph of ten sentences, describing the picture. Tell what the occasion is, where everyone is gathered, what gifts the various members of the family offer, what Mme Dupont's reaction is to the gifts, what the family will do afterwards, etc. Vary your sentences.
10 points

LA FAMILLE DUPONT
Claude Dupont
Monique Dupont
Françoise
Vincent
Frédérique
Xavier

_____

_____

_____

_____

_____

_____

SCORE [ ]

6. This part is optional. You may earn an extra four points. Complete the conversation between Françoise and Vincent, who are deciding what to buy for their mother's birthday.

FRANÇOISE Alors, qu'est-ce qu'on lui achète?

VINCENT _____

FRANÇOISE On pourrait lui offrir un sac.

VINCENT _____

FRANÇOISE On lui achète des gants?

VINCENT _____

FRANÇOISE Ça coûte cher le parfum?

VINCENT _____

SCORE [ ]

Summary Test after Unit 24

1. In the following paragraph, some verbs have been left in the infinitive form. Decide whether they should be in the future or the conditional, and write the correct forms in the spaces provided below.
20 points

(Suzanne écrit un petit mot à son amie pour lui dire qu'elle va faire bientôt un voyage au Sénégal avec sa famille.)

Nous partirons en bateau au Sénégal quand nous (avoir[1]) nos passeports. Si ma mère n'était pas froussarde, on (prendre[2]) l'avion. On y (passer[3]) une semaine si tout va bien. Tu (pouvoir[4]) venir avec nous si tu étais libre. Si tu venais, ce (être[5]) formidable! Nous (s'amuser[6]) bien ensemble! Je t'achèterai un souvenir quand nous (visiter[7]) les marchés à Dakar. Après avoir marchandé avec les marchands, bien sûr! Ils (être[8]) tenaces, mais c'est moi qui (gagner[9]). Quand je (revenir[10]), je te dévoilerai la vie exotique de l'Afrique.

1. _____   6. _____

2. _____   7. _____

3. _____   8. _____

4. _____   9. _____

5. _____   10. _____

SCORE [   ]

2. Complete the chart with three countries of your choice in the indicated areas of the world. Use the definite article **le, la,** or **les.**
12 points

	L'AFRIQUE	L'EUROPE	L'AMERIQUE DU NORD
le nom du pays			
la langue (les langues)			
les habitants			
la capitale			

SCORE [   ]

3. Write a sentence, comparing the two TV shows. Use the correct form of the adjective in parentheses. The symbols indicate whether you are to write a statement of equality (=) or inequality (> more, < less).
12 points

EXAMPLE:

les histoires d'amour > les documentaires   (impressionnant)

Les histoires d'amour sont plus impressionnantes que les documentaires.

12. les publicités = les jeux   (amusant)

_____

13. les émissions de variétés < le journal télévisé   (ennuyeux)

_____

_____

14. les séries (feuilletons) > les films de science-fiction   (intéressant)

_____

_____

15. les documentaires > les émissions sportives   (bon)

_____

SCORE [   ]

4. Write a TV commercial for the following product.
6 points

16. _____

_____

_____

SCORE [   ]

Summary Test after Unit 24 (continued)

5. Rewrite the sentences, adding the superlative of the given adjective. Remember to put the adjective in its correct form and place.
10 points
EXAMPLE: C'est un appareil. (cher) (plus)

C'est l'appareil le plus cher.

17. Le problème, c'est la pollution. (sérieux) (plus)

_____

18. L'enfant a pris la pomme. (grand) (plus)

_____

19. C'est elle qui a proposé l'idée. (original) (moins)

_____

20. Elle choisit la couleur. (joli) (moins)

_____

21. Nous avons suivi le chemin. (rapide) (plus)

_____

SCORE [ ]

6. Imagine that you are going to visit the Slim family in Tunisia this summer. Write a paragraph of five sentences about your trip.
10 points

_____

_____

_____

_____

_____

SCORE [ ]

7. Complete the following conversation by filling in the correct interrogative pronouns: **qui est-ce qui, qui est-ce que, qu'est-ce qui, qu'est-ce que, qui,** or **quoi.**
12 points

    —Samedi prochain, c'est son anniversaire!

22. —De _____? —De Viviane.

    —On va donner une surprise-partie? —Bien sûr!

23. —_____ nous allons inviter? —Toute la bande!

24. —_____ nous allons lui acheter comme cadeau?

25. —Je ne sais pas. _____ lui ferait plaisir?

    —Elle adore les boucles d'oreille.

26. —Avec _____ est-ce qu'on va les acheter?

    —On peut emprunter de l'argent aux parents.

27. —_____ a un électrophone qui marche bien?

    —Philippe. Il vient d'en acheter un nouveau.

SCORE [ ]

8. Write a vocabulary word that fits the given definition. Pay careful attention to any object pronouns that provide clues. Use an article before each noun.
18 points

EXAMPLE: On la parle. *une langue*

28. Les avions y atterrissent et décollent.

    _____

29. On la règle quand elle est floue.

    _____

30. On y garde son argent.

    _____

31. On y va pour faire un tour sur les manèges.

    _____

32. C'est la plus grande épreuve sportive annuelle.

    _____

33. Quand on fait des exercices au sol, on la plie souvent.

    _____

34. Quelques parents en donnent chaque semaine ou chaque mois à leurs enfants.

    _____

35. On la regarde à la télévision.

    _____

36. On l'a souvent quand on est sur le grand huit.

    _____

G 5
H 6
I 7
J 8

SCORE [ ]